LIFE IN THE ESTROGEN-FREE ZONE

LIFE IN THE ESTROGEN-FREE ZONE

HUMOR AND HEARTFELT WISDOM FROM BOY MOMS

Michelle Rayburn
and Friends

Foreword by Pam Farrel

Life in the Estrogen-Free Zone: Humor and Heartfelt Wisdom from Boy Moms

ISBN: 978-0-9885286-8-0
Published by Faith Creativity Life Books
fclbooks.com

This work depicts actual events in the life of the authors as truthfully as recollection permits. Neither the publisher nor the writers are engaged in rendering professional advice or services to the reader. The ideas, suggestions, and methods provided in this book are not intended as a substitute for seeking professional guidance.

Compiled and edited by Michelle Rayburn – michellerayburn.com
Foreword by Pam Farrel – love-wise.com
Cover, typesetting, and eBook design by Michelle Rayburn – missionandmedia.com
Photos and illustrations: Storyblocks images

TO OUR SONS, the testosterone-fueled blessings in our lives. This book is dedicated to your knack for turning every moment into an adventure, reminding us that laughter and a little mayhem are the secret ingredients to a remarkable legacy—and the source of a few gray hairs.

Contents

Foreword by Pam Farrel ix

LITTLES

The Birth of a Boy Mom - *Michelle Rayburn* 3
If You Know a Tired Mama - *Avonlea Q. Krueger* 9
A Stitch or Two in Time - *Gina Stinson* 15
My Plans Meet God's Double Plot Twist - *Ginny Dent Brant* 21
Stumbling, Fumbling Mom - *Joni Topper* 29
Building Faith—From What-Ifs to What Is - *Melissa Meyer* 35
Bubble Wrap, Broken Bones, and Blessings - *Michelle Rayburn* 41
Wearing the Dad Hat—Or Face - *Valerie McNulty* 47

GROWING BOYS

From Foster to Forever - *Betty Predmore* 55
You've Been Drafted - *Stacy Sanchez* 61
This Rough Patch, Then Strawberries Come June - *Abigail Wallace* 67
I'm Raising a Boy and Have Oodles of Questions! - *Melissa Meyer* 73
10 Things I Love About Being a Boy Mom - *Michelle Rayburn* 79
Video Games, Bad Dudes, and Mom Anxiety - *Abigail Wallace* 85
Raising, Rivaling, and Resolving - *Kolleen Lucariello* 93

Moving, Moods, Mudbugs, and Maturing - *Gina Stinson* 101
It's the #Boymom Life for Me! - *Stacy Sanchez* 107

TEENS

Four by Camper and Three by Canoe - *Michelle Rayburn* 115
Defusing Fear and Exploding Faith - *Pam Fields* 121
Where the Wild Things Were - *Becky Melby* 127
Head Held High - *Denise Loock* 133
So-and-So's Mom - *Joni Topper* 139
Midnight Snacks - *Gina Stinson* 147
Holey Socks, Holy Work - *Michelle Rayburn* 153

YOUNG MEN

Short Time, Far-Reaching Influence - *Rhonda Stoppe* 161
A Sparkling Surprise for a Single Mom - *Christina Ryan Claypool* 167
The Winking Elvis and a Type A Soldier - *Kim Cusimano* 173
Forgiveness Sets Us Free - *Maureen Miller* 179
Learners and Leaders Who Love God - *Pam Farrel* 187
From Nest to Next - *Michelle Rayburn* 195

Final Thoughts 201

Foreword

Pam Farrel

I VALUE AND APPRECIATE THE HEART and vision of Michelle Rayburn and this volume packed with power, practicality, and promise. *Life in the Estrogen-Free Zone: Humor and Heartfelt Wisdom from Boy Moms* will be a breath of fresh air of hope and help. As a mother of three sons, I sought out the wisdom of other moms of boys who had been there. Moms who:

- Are overwhelmed with a house full of testosterone that feels so different from her estrogen-oriented worldview.
- Find rocks, frogs, snails, and bugs in the pockets of grass-stained jeans.
- Play catcher when her boy wants to learn to pitch or throw a ball.
- Discover her boys rappelling down the stairwell from their second-story bedroom.
- Find themselves the smallest and shortest person in the household.
- Roll down the van windows even on a cold winter's day because the van is packed with sweaty athletes.

- Go to the grocery store AGAIN for milk, snacks, and more protein.
- Referee (and often give first aid) in the backyard skate-park, flag-football game, or bike jump.
- Beg for less dirt and mud and more peace and quiet.
- Pray for wisdom about helping her son(s) navigate what it means to be masculine in a very confusing world.
- Long to teach their sons to be godly leaders with a compassionate heart and wisdom for decisions.

I am grateful to God for verses compelling other mothers who have walked my path to share their journeys:

> As iron sharpens iron, so a friend sharpens a friend. (Proverbs 27:17)

> Similarly, teach the older women to live in a way that honors God. They must not slander others or be heavy drinkers. Instead, they should teach others what is good. These older women must train the younger women to love their husbands and their children, to live wisely and be pure, to work in their homes, to do good, and to be submissive to their husbands. Then they will not bring shame on the word of God. (Titus 2:3–5)

> When she speaks, her words are wise, and she gives instructions with kindness. (Proverbs 31:26)

We need each other, Mom. I am thankful for Michelle and all the mothers who have shared their real-life, authentic stories of life with their sons. I am grateful for the honesty, the humor, and the practical, godly wisdom these moms share.

I am also grateful for what we learn from their sons, their boys of all ages. I have also learned much from my own sons. Let me just share a God moment from the mouths of each of my three sons.

MY ELDEST, WHEN HE WAS only about two years old, was like most preschoolers in that if you watched a video once, you watched it a thousand times! Brock loved the "Jesus" movie, and he would watch it all the way through the pray-along at the end, which invites the audience to receive Christ as Savior.

At a family camp where my husband and I were teaching, Brock was tired of the childcare time and wanted to hang out with Mom and Dad. It was my turn at the podium, so Bill took Brock on a nature walk. Brock began to recite, almost word for word, the verses from *The Jesus Film*.

Bill, who later told me he'd thought Brock must be an early spiritual bloomer, asked him, "Son, do you want to ask Jesus into your life?"

Brock answered, "No, when Jesus gets out of the Bible, then I will ask him into my heart."

When Bill had Brock share this story with me at bedtime, I knew God was giving my husband and me our marching orders as parents: make Jesus REAL!

The following year, I was with our boys in a cabin with another youth pastor's wife while our husbands oversaw the teens from our mega church. At bedtime, Brock began what we all know as a kosher delay of bedtime, asking Mom important questions—especially about God. Brock was asking things like "Who made the earth?" and "Why did God make animals?" and other questions that I felt qualified to field.

Then three-year-old Brock asked, "If God is good, and Satan is evil, and God made everything, did God create evil?"

Yikes! I am pretty sure that is a seminary-level Bible question! I knew that night that I needed to keep growing in my own walk with God because there would be tough questions on my son's heart on the road ahead. I needed to be able to live out these verses:

> You must worship Christ as Lord of your life. And if someone asks about your hope as a believer, always be ready to explain it. (1 Peter 3:15)

> Preach the word of God. Be prepared, whether the time is favorable or not. Patiently correct, rebuke, and encourage your people with good teaching. (2 Timothy 4:2)

My second-born son, who had ADD/ADHD, tagged me on the way to teach at a family camp when he was in fifth grade. In our bestselling book *Men Are Like Waffles, Women Are Like Spaghetti*, we tell a story from our honeymoon where I was standing in front of a mirror, criticizing my twenty-year-old self. God prompted Bill to come and wrap me in his arms and say, "Let me be your mirror. If you need to know how beautiful, godly, and capable you are, come see me. Let me be your mirror." In our seminars, we go on to share the power of encouraging words.

I realized on the boat over to the island that in the packing of everything we needed to take our family of five plus my mom to a remote family camp, I had forgotten the mirror prop for that story. I began to criticize myself and ride myself for my forgetfulness out loud, and my Zach took my face in his dirty, grimy hands and said, "Mom, let me be your mirror. If you need to know what a good mom you are, come see me. I will tell you that you are a good mom."

Boom. Mic drop.

We all laughed at the obvious message from heaven to my heart.

Lastly, our youngest is a very sensitive soul. He is also very perceptive, and his joy of learning appeared early in life. He was also a preschooler when my speaking and book writing experienced explosive growth (accompanied by ever-pressing deadlines). While I was trying to finish one more paragraph, Caleb was trying to get my attention. There was a bug on the sidewalk that he wanted me to see. He enthusiastically tapped my shoulder and repeated, "Mom, Mom, Mom!" Yet it was not breaking through my focus and concentration.

Finally, he put his little preschool hands on my cheeks and said, "Wisten to me, Mom. Wisten to me! If you don't come now, you will miss it!"

This little guy was God's messenger to remind me to embrace living in the moment, or I might miss some precious memories with my boys.

Yes, you will learn much from other mothers from the pages of this wonderful book. You will even learn from the testosterone-filled sons of these diligent, engaged yet imperfect mothers. But you will also learn from God. I have been praying that we each receive a postcard from our Abba Father, our own sticky note from heaven to our hearts and home. So, get your pen ready to underline the wisdom, and pull out your multi-colored sticky notes to tab the inspiring places, the stories, and the life-giving truths on the pages ahead.

Being a mom of sons is a treasured, holy journey, and this book is a welcome compass, pointing to the true north on the path ahead.

Pam Farrel

PAM FARREL is the bestselling author of sixty books, including *The 10 Best Decisions a Parent Can Make* and *10 Questions Kids Ask About Sex* as well as the Amazon bestselling *Discovering the Bible* series of creative Bible studies. She and her husband, Bill, have been happily married for forty-three years and co-direct Love-Wise ministry. They are parents to three now-grown sons, three daughters-in-law, and seven grandkids. The Farrels have downsized and now make their home on a live-aboard boat docked in Southern California. **Love-Wise.com**

Littles

The Birth of a Boy Mom

Michelle Rayburn

"IT LOOKS LIKE A GRENADE went off down there." Those were the words that began our parenting adventure as my husband, Phil, had a little fraternity party with the doctor at the end of the bed while I pushed my eyeballs out of their sockets as I bore down with massive contractions. The point was to push a baby out of my bottom, but that wasn't progressing as well as the party between the only two guys in the room—unless you count the one that was the *real* center of attention. But we didn't know his sex yet.

While nurses held a leg on each side, and the doctor attempted to artfully create some sort of suturable episiotomy in my nether regions, there was a camaraderie of the brotherhood that I didn't understand happening between the two men waiting to catch our eight-pound, thirteen-ounce, cone-headed blessing.

In their defense, we had all been working on the process for nearly eighteen hours—well, I had been working, and they were pretty much observing. Also, in Phil's defense, tactfulness has never superseded an opportunity for him to make a joke, so I should have expected this.

Baby Makes Three—or Four

"Will you have to give her a transfusion after this?" Phil was not about to give up on the momentum he had going.

"Hey guys, over here. I can't feel my legs. Have you noticed the nurses? I'm a puppet without strings right now."

I was grateful for the epidural but had to watch the contractions on the bedside monitor and wait for the tightening sensation in my back to know when to push. Sometimes epidurals do their job *too* well.

A few more snips and a couple of pushes, and Dallas, our first baby boy, finally entered the world. This was the start of testosterone domination at our house.

"Is this normal? Will his head stay like that?" Phil has always loved asking questions to which he already knows the answer.

Fast forward a bit. Two years later, on the same day, and within the same hour of the day, baby boy number two was born. I know. I'm organized like that. Austin (no geographical affiliation on the name choices) completed our little family of four, and I decided that if God blessed us with sons, I didn't need to keep pumping out kiddos until I got one with pigtails—no disrespect to families who have more than two, or even more than ten children.

With both births, we had the option of having Phil spend the night on a cot in the hospital, but if we chose this option, the baby also had to stay in our room. I opted to let Daddy drive home, even though it was the wee hours of the morning by the time my stitches were finished, and I'd had some toast and applesauce and was ready to settle down. We decided the nurses were exceptionally qualified to watch babies all night, and I desperately needed some sleep.

I also needed to let my eyeballs recess back to where they belonged. I'm sure my crossed eyes weren't as noticeable as it seemed they were to me. I wanted a root beer and to sleep for a hundred years. At least I got the root beer.[1]

---

1. Michelle Rayburn, *Classic Marriage: Staying in Love as Your Odometer Climbs* (New Auburn, WI: Faith Creativity Life Books, 2020), 63–64.

Baby Changes ~~Nothing~~ Everything

There are extensive books available to explain what to expect while pregnant and what to expect in the first year. They cover spitting up, constipation, prepping the family pet, lactation, snake bites and spider bites, and babyproofing. But they miss a lot.

Where are the chapters on falling asleep as soon as you try to watch a movie together, children barfing in the sheets of *your* bed, getting parental sleep in two-minute increments, and the impossibility of losing the baby weight while surviving on hotdogs and frozen pizza?

For dads, where are the CliffsNotes on receiving zero attention while your wife smooches the cheeks off your spawn? Or on precisely how much touching stay-at-home mommies can tolerate after a day with the kids? And where are the books on being patient when Daddy wants to go hunting, but Mommy is a raging hormonal maniac who doesn't trust herself for one more minute with your mini-me?

> Life as a mom is wonderful and new, but let's face reality. Babies change everything.

BC (before children), I experienced baby fever whenever one of my friends brought a new bundle of joy into the world. There is this maternal instinct that kicks in when a woman holds a baby. No matter what friends tell us or how many times we see YouTube videos of babies having diaper blowouts, impressive spit-ups, or colicky fits, and no matter how sleep-deprived our friends look, there comes a point when many of us think our life will *never* be complete without a child in it.[2]

Let's have a moment of silence for the life we used to have.

Amen.

---

2. *Classic Marriage*, 63–64.

Life as a mom is wonderful and new, but let's face reality. Babies change everything. There are no lazy Saturday mornings if Junior wants to breastfeed at 5:00 a.m. The sewing room is now a nursery, and your once-treasured hobby supplies now live in rubber totes on basement shelves. (You'll find your pretty papers, fabrics, markers, and ribbons someday when you're packing to move.) Someone will throw up just before a road trip or spike a fever on the night before you hop on a plane for Disney. And you'll have to make the excruciating decisions to answer the question: Should we still go?

Baby Brings Joy

Not every change is tragic. And that's why getting a puppy will never turn off baby fever. Ask me how I know. It's why we don't care what it will do to our old life. Somewhere inside, there's an instinct that tells us to trust the process, that it will be beautiful, that there are indescribable joys to be discovered.

I had no idea how my heart would explode the first time my son said, "Momma." Or that I could love him so much that I wanted to eat him. That sounds disturbing. Maybe it was the oxytocin and estrogen overload, but I wanted to devour his chubby fingers, squishy thighs, and button nose—and a Yale psychology study said saying things like "I could eat him up" is normal.[3] Whew!

I can look back now that both boys have left the nest and started their own families. But several decades ago, my whole life was about diapering their bottoms, spoon-feeding prunes for constipation, and wiping boogers with a tissue—okay, sometimes my shirt. But this momma's heart will never forget the feeling when they uttered their first giggle or blew raspberries back to me. Or the smell of a freshly washed baby in jammies. Or the sound of cooing over a monitor.

And I kind of wish I could give my former self a little advice: Don't perm your hair; the photos in their baby albums will be hard to take

3. "'Tears of Joy' May Help Us Maintain Emotional Balance," Association for Psychological Science (website), November 12, 2014, https://www.psychologicalscience.org/news/releases/tears-of-joy-may-help-us-maintain-emotional-balance.html.

seriously. Hold on to those mom jeans; they will come back again. Relax. You're doing great.

Baby Inspires a Sorority

Hey, momma holding this book, I see you. Relax. You're doing great. Feeling a bit frazzled? We're right here with you. Do you melt at seeing your little boy dressed up in mini man-jeans and a buttoned shirt? Been there. Do you secretly love being nap trapped in the rocker? Me too! Those cuddles are so sweet.

It's been so long since I've found a teeny-tiny sock inside a leg of my laundered flannel pajamas. Any trauma from labor and delivery has long faded. I don't budget for diapers or formula anymore. But over the years, I've discovered that the role of mother morphs but doesn't diminish. And it comes with automatic membership in the best club ever.

I've discovered that the role of mother morphs but doesn't diminish. And it comes with automatic membership in the best club ever.

I was never cool enough for a college sorority, but now I've joined a sisterhood I can handle. Every time a doctor says, "It's a boy," another mother joins a sorority of boy moms who brighten when they see a social media post with #boymom attached. We *know*.

She can lock eyes with a mom across a fast-food restaurant and convey all the feels about that meltdown the other's son is having. Her smile says, *You've got this, Mom.* She's among others who get how fierce love for the tiny human with XY chromosomes can't be put into words while, at the same time, he also tries her patience like no other.

A sorority lifeline quietly pulses beneath the pounding heartbeat of the frat party raucous from husbands and sons. Like the Virgin

Mary, each mother keeps things in her heart and thinks about them often.[4] And when she gets together with fellow boy moms, she revels in their company, treasures their wisdom, and refuels her soul.

Welcome to the sorority.

MICHELLE RAYBURN is an author and podcast host who helps others find hope in the trashy stuff of life. She has an MA in ministry leadership and writes Christian living books, humor, and Bible studies. Together with her husband, they've raised two sons and gained two daughters-in-law—plus three granddaughters (go estrogen team!) and a grandson. Dark chocolate, an iced coffee, and a good book in the hammock top Michelle's favorites list. **michellerayburn.com**

4. Luke 2:19

If You Know a Tired Mama

Avonlea Q. Krueger

SHE CAME ONE NIGHT WITH a raw chicken. I knew she'd be staying a while. And I welcomed her into the quiet of our little stone house. John was away in London. Or Edinburgh, perhaps. And even with the woods and the beaches to walk, the days and nights grew long, just Baby and me.

How to Love a Tired Mama

Soon the oven warmed the kitchen, and smells spread through the house. She sat with me while I fed and changed him. She spoke with me, listened as if she'd nowhere else to go. And when Baby was down, and our bellies were full, she sat a bit longer just to chat over tea.

A few months on and we were moving south, leaving Inverness for the hills of Perthshire, and she came back. She and another friend, as if it were nothing. They came with boxes, newspapers, and bags, and within days the house was wrapped and packed. It was nothing I could have done on my own, not me and Baby, who climbed in and out of boxes, unpacking what I'd packed.

And I was grateful, oh so grateful, for their help. But it was more than the job, of course, more than helping me move house. It was also their time, their laughter, their there-ness that spoke volumes to my tired mama's heart.

How to Love a Tired Mama—Even More

It's been eight years, but I'm still talking. Still telling what happened—what she did—with as much excitement as if I'd just stepped off the train.

It was January. Charlie, my fourth son, was just a month old—still waking often, still calling me from shallow sleep to hold him, me back-bent and weary as I rocked, rocked, and tried to keep my head from nodding as I fed him off to sleep. January, and I was still recovering from his birth, still tender and swollen, still feeling lost as I waded through the emotions that come with newborns and returning to Scotland to visit after three long years. January, and despite craving sleep like an addict, I felt anxious to do some shopping for the belated Christmas we'd be sharing with my family when we returned to the States.

I couldn't drive, but there were trains. I decided to catch one, just me and Charlie, to Inverness, where we used to live and where one can find such delights as Primark, Debenhams, and Marks & Spencer. I was set to do the return trip in a day, but the night before, I spoke to a friend from our old church. A trendy grandmother with a soft young voice, smiling eyes, and a penchant for the color blue. She convinced me—without much effort—that Charlie and I should stay the night. Have two days in town instead of one.

> Just a night in that house, and I felt rejuvenated. Encouraged. Loved. Ministered to in every way.

The trip began disastrously. I spent half the time trying to ignore the stressful cries of a newborn and the other half in the dressing room feeding him and changing his nappy. I would have had to go home empty-handed, frustrated, in tears. But instead came my friend with her car to meet me and whisk Charlie and me off to her home for a hot dinner (she held the baby while I ate!), endless cups of tea (she said I must keep my strength up), and a heart-to-heart conversation in a soft chair (I sat while she bathed the baby).

And that's only the beginning. I haven't yet mentioned the fruit and water bottles she'd put in my room in the event I needed a late-night snack, the electric blanket that had been turned on to keep my bed warm and waiting, or the new home décor magazines that she set out in case I wanted to take a look. It was Disneyland for new moms. I laid my head on my crisp white pillow that night with a smile on my face and peace in my heart. Just a night in that house, and I felt rejuvenated. Encouraged. Loved. Ministered to in every way.

And I could say my friend is just like that. Just the sort of person to convince you she liked sleeping on the floor and that you *really should* have her bed. And perhaps that's a little bit true. But if you've seen her Bible, then you'll know it's also a little bit more than that. Bookmarks sticking out like porcupine quills. Notes added to the margins in her tiny, dancing hand.

She spends a great deal of time with that book, I gather. Probably a great deal of time on her knees too. And somehow, in a way that surpasses all comprehension, spending time with that book has the power to transform us. To help us stop thinking of our own needs and see the needs of others. Help us see what a teary-eyed, bone-weary mama needs more than anything else.

If You Are a Tired Mama

Usually, it was fish and chips that our friends offered to bring. Crispy, battered haddock and thick-cut fries doused with vinegar and a sprinkling of salt. Picked up from the chippy on their way over. I'd start to tidy but would remind myself not to worry too much. Just a quick wipe of the bathrooms and a fresh hand towel (one of my personal hospitality must-dos) would suffice.

There wasn't much point in frantically scooping LEGO pieces into toy bins or straightening out the sofa cushions. Our friends did, after all, have three little boys who'd be joining our two (at that time), and I knew I could expect the five of them to make quick work of emptying the wicker toy basket and turning the sofa into a pirate ship.

After the ketchup-soaked fish and chips papers had been cleared away, and the children were in the other room hard at play, the adults would gather round the dining room table, within earshot of the littles in case someone got a bump or there was a lesson on sharing that needed to be learned. There'd be tea then, and some little nibbles, and the stresses of life would dissipate as we talked and shared, the fire crackling at our backs. They'd stay past bedtime, but we didn't mind.

They were our last-minute friends. The spontaneous ones. We loved it, and it went both ways. We phoned once on our way home from a day of picnicking and wading in the rock pools of St Andrews. And we were invited to "tea" (the evening meal in many parts of Scotland). There were probably toys everywhere. Crumbs on the floor. Some sprinkles on the toilet seat. But I don't remember. What I do remember is the lamb chops smothered in curry paste—and the homemade sweet potato fries sprinkled with salt and hot pepper seeds. I remember Mary's smile. I remember there was cake.

A mama doesn't mind it. Not one little bit. Doesn't mind balancing her cup of tea as she picks her way over the minefield of toys to make her way to your couch.

Later on, Mary and I nursed cups of milky tea beside the patio doors while the men took the children into the cool autumn air to play on the trampoline. Two tired mamas. We talked. We laughed. We shared our hearts so that the other knew how to pray. We felt stronger. We knew love. Because, you see, a mama doesn't mind it. Not one little bit. Doesn't mind balancing her cup of tea as she picks her way over the minefield of toys to make her way to your couch. Isn't fazed by having to grab a wad of toilet roll to wipe sprinkles from your toilet seat. Has selective vision when it comes to the pile of dishes in your sink.

She didn't come to inspect your house. She didn't come to give you extra work. She came for the friendship. The laughter. She came to see *you*.

Friendship and laughter bring sanity. Clarity. They help us see that most of the chaos is normal and we're not the only ones going through it all. God made us that way. To bear one another's burdens. To celebrate together. And I have to remind myself of this often:

> My desire is to bless, not to impress.
> Laughter is made brighter,
> and tears are made lighter
> when there's cake.

Cake, and of course, a hot cup of tea. And so, even if you *are* a tired mama, don't let this stop you from letting others into your house, especially if they are a tired mama too.

AVONLEA Q. KRUEGER is a graduate of Hope College in Holland, Michigan. She also studied in Scotland, where she met her husband, John, and began her ties with the British Isles. After eight wonderful years abroad, Avonlea currently resides in a big old brick house in West Michigan. She is the author of the novel *The House on Cherry Street* and has a passion for homeschooling and inspiring women's faith. Connect with her at **happylittlesigh.com**.

A Stitch or Two in Time

Gina Stinson

I COULD HAVE PREDICTED LIFE WITH Tucker was going to be exciting when he was born with a mullet. I giggle every time I remember my husband shaving Tucker's head with an electric razor within two weeks of his birth. I am not sure which looked more comical—the mullet or the military-style flattop! Poor guy. Adventures began early for him.

When our boys are young, they lack the common sense to know how difficult or dangerous something is. The life skills needed to make good decisions just aren't developed yet. It's no fault of their own. As life moves on, they grow, and parents attempt to nurture good habits and safety in hopes that their boys will be responsible. It's every parent's dream to keep them safe and free from harm. But some boys attract adventure more than others. Such is the case with my son.

If a Mom Makes a Dream Plan

I accepted a job offer to work from home when Tucker was about a year old. We had recently moved to a new community, and I was trying to be a stay-at-home mom for as long as I could after he was born. The job was perfect, and within a couple of days of accepting the position, I had designed a small office area in the corner of our playroom and was ready to go to work.

My plan was all so clear to me. I would wake up an hour before Tucker. I'd work while he was still sleeping. Then when he awoke, I would tenderly walk into his room, lift him from his crib for morning snuggles and begin the day with him. We'd play. I would read him, *Brown Bear, Brown Bear, What Do You See?* He'd take a morning nap, and I would get back to work. He'd wake in time for a healthy lunch of veggies and protein and then enjoy some music and a little TV time.

I'd have the laundry started and do a little picking up while he played quietly in his playpen. He'd enjoy a mid-afternoon nap and wake just in time for playtime with Dad. I'd work again and also prepare a delicious home-cooked meal.

I should have known this dream would quickly fade.

I should have known this dream would quickly fade.

If You Give a Mom a Minute

Day three of my new job began with a fussy boy with a snotty nose. He was inconsolable. Puppets couldn't make him happy. His favorite bear couldn't make him happy. His favorite book couldn't make him happy. After two hours of fussing and crying, we rocked and sang all the songs he knew, and he seemed to be feeling better. He played at my feet while I began working for the day. I filed away some papers before lunch and was feeling pretty good about things. "I can do this," I thought.

At lunch, he fell asleep—probably from all the crying and fit-throwing from earlier in the day. I laid him down in his bed and silently hoped to make up some of the time I had missed that morning with the new job. I didn't want to disappoint my boss. Thankfully, Tucker slept for over two hours, giving me plenty of time to make up for lost time.

When he awoke from his nap, we snuggled, and he seemed happy to play at my feet again. Only this time, he pulled up on the corner of the metal filing cabinet and cut his head. Instantly, blood poured from his head, and I was a wreck. Scrambling, I called my husband

and assured him Tucker was probably going to bleed to death, and he needed to hurry home.

He rushed home from his office just a mile away. We piled in the car and headed to our local minor care. Like Humpty Dumpty, Tucker's head was glued back together, and within hours, he was acting like nothing had happened. He had no idea what he had put his mother through!

If a Boy Takes a Bath

Less than a week later, with weather forecasters predicting an ice storm, I decided to give the kids an early bath while Bruce fixed dinner. The plan: feed the kids, watch a movie in front of the fireplace, and put them to bed early. If we could pull this off, it would be a parent win! Savannah got her bath, and then I put Tucker in the tub. He splashed in the shallow water and played for a few minutes. I turned to grab the towel to put around him, and instantly, he was standing and holding on to the faucet for dear life. In what seemed like slow motion, he slipped and hit his chin. Blood poured everywhere. I screamed for Bruce, who level-headedly took over the situation.

At the time, we had a veterinarian in our church. Since the roads were icing over, Bruce thought he would call him up and see if he would look at Tucker's chin to see if it needed stitches. We didn't want to be on the road if it wasn't necessary. Looking back on this, I am not sure why we thought calling the vet was a good idea, but nonetheless, Dr. Wilkens assured us we needed medical attention and offered us his vehicle to drive the twenty miles to the nearest hospital. Seven stitches later, we were bringing our boy back home.

If You Give a Boy a Fort Kit

When Tucker was four years old, we gave him a homemade fort kit for Christmas. We included a flat sheet, six clamps, two battery-operated lanterns, beef jerky, rope, and a sleeping bag. Our vision: create a fort outside. His vision: turn the playroom into Fort Central. Due to bad weather, his vision came to fruition.

Picture it: dining chairs clamped with a sheet, lit up with the fluorescent light of the lanterns, beef jerky wafting in the air. It would be any little boy's haven. But Tucker took it to the next level. The rope included in the kit needed to serve a purpose, so he tied it around the legs of furniture to create "traps" for people to get across without tripping. What had once been a well-decorated den now appeared to be somewhat of a survival game. He could not have been prouder of himself. Joy spread across his face. He had created a course he was sure would be a challenge to all who crossed it. I'm not sure he was wrong.

During that Christmas season, we all maneuvered our way around that room, allowing for the silliness of the traps to remain up and running for a couple of weeks. We tripped, stumbled, fell, and laughed a lot during those times. Tucker's sense of fun and adventure kept a smile on all of our faces. He was especially proud of himself.

If a Mom Embraces Adventure

Remarkably, since Tucker's early interaction with stitches and glue, he's remained somewhat unscathed by all the adventures he's taken. He's given me plenty of other reasons to check my heart rate, though. As a little one, his tactics and shenanigans wore me out physically. Keeping up with him was a constant rhythm of redirection and discipline. Sometimes I did this well, and sometimes I failed. Many nights I fell asleep wondering if I was doing anything right.

I learned so much about my need for God during those younger days.

I learned so much about my need for God during those younger days. I learned about patience and love, but I also learned about being intentional and meeting Tucker where he was rather than thinking he understood all the adult words and phrases. His little mind didn't always understand the danger he placed himself in (all the climbing and jumping and picking up gross insects), and in all honesty, sometimes my mind would overreact. I would embrace the worst possible outcome instead of thinking and acting logically. Everything was not an emergency.

That's where God taught me to trust him. I could take all the precautions. I could order our days. I could love him the best I knew how. But if I didn't trust God to do what was best for Tucker, was I really trusting him? I had to let go. I loved Tucker to pieces. Still do. But God loves him more. When Tucker is in adventurous situations, even dangerous, I am learning that trusting God's love for Tucker is better than my own love for him.

Those years flew by. Those toddler moments are just a stitch in time. The adventures and obstacles he will face now are more than a homemade fort kit or a few stitches on his chin. This mom will continue to pray all those prayers for his safety, but mostly I'll pray that I will trust God with Tucker and that Tucker will trust God too.

After years of living in fear and defeat, **GINA STINSON** is reclaiming every day for God's glory. She's a pastor's wife of thirty years and mom of two young adults. Gina is a storyteller writer who enjoys retelling wonderful ways God is at work. She's incredibly easy to locate on social media or at **ginastinson.com**. Otherwise, you'll find her at the hobby shop wandering the yarn aisle looking for inspiration for her next project.

My Plans Meet God's Double Plot Twist

Ginny Dent Brant

MY HUSBAND, ALTON, AND I were thrilled when I gave birth to our first child—a son. He entered the world at nearly ten pounds. He was perfect in every way. When he turned two, we began planning for another bundle of joy. Realizing this might be it for us, I searched and discovered a book called *How to Determine the Sex of Your Child*. Within minutes, I was speed-reading this book for suggestions on how to produce a girl. We already had a boy. I was determined to have a girl!

You can imagine the look on my husband's face a few months later when I summoned him home immediately. "Why now?" he asked.

"According to my calendar, the book says now is the time to produce a girl!" I responded.

"I don't work that way!" my husband teased. "You need to wine and dine me first." He was home in a flash. Just a few months later, I was pregnant. It appeared my plan was successful.

Another Miscarriage?

Unfortunately, at ten weeks, I began spotting, and I went directly from work to my doctor's office. My mind flashed back to a previous miscarriage. "Please, Lord," I sighed. "Not again."

Dr. Kulbersh immediately pulled out an ultrasound machine and began scoping my belly. He stopped abruptly and left the room. I could hear my doctor and his partner, Dr. Plyler, mumbling outside the door. Did I hear giggling? They appeared oblivious to my agony. I was holding back tears. I'd been in this very room when I heard the shocking news: "No heartbeat."

A few minutes later, both doctors entered the room and continued the ultrasound.

"Do you see this?" Dr. Kulbersh asked.

"Yes," I replied. "It looks like a mouth opening and closing."

"It's a heartbeat, and that's a good thing," he said. "Now look over here."

"What's that?" I asked.

"It's another heartbeat," he said, grinning ear to ear.

"I don't understand. What are you saying?"

"Double carriage—not miscarriage," Dr. Plyler blurted with a gust of laughter. Then Dr. Kulbersh joined his gleeful duet. Their laughter lightened my misery.

"Twins!" Dr. Kulbersh explained.

Tears rolled down my cheeks. "You mean everything's okay?"

Tears rolled down my cheeks. "You mean everything's okay?"

"Yes. It appears your symptoms were caused by your babies growing rapidly. It's probably the reason you're spotting and having morning sickness. Double babies, double hormones."

There was a skip in my step as I walked to my car and drove home. My husband and his mom anxiously greeted me at the front door.

"No miscarriage this time. Double carriage instead." The puzzled look on their faces let me know I was not the only slow-thinking person that day. My husband threw his arms around me, and my mother-in-law danced a jig. We'd received a double blessing from God.

A High-Risk Pregnancy

Dr. Kulbersh insisted my husband come to my next checkup. After a thorough examination, he took us to his office for some candid advice. "Twin pregnancies are high risk," he said. "I need to see Ginny more often to make sure everything is progressing without any complications."

Then he opened a book and showed us a profile picture of a woman pregnant with twins.

"Oh my," my husband gasped. "Will my wife look like this?"

"Probably," he replied. "Even maternity clothes may not fit. And she may not carry them full-term. Most moms don't. It's best that Ginny carry these twins as close to term as possible. The weight of a double pregnancy usually initiates early labor. I may have to take her off her feet at about twenty weeks."

"But I have to work to pay the bills and carry the insurance," I reminded.

"You'll do what I say if you don't want these twins struggling in neonatal care," he said emphatically.

I continued to grow rapidly and had monthly ultrasounds. After the fourth ultrasound, my doctor informed me that Twin A was a boy.

"Oh, wonderful," I replied. "As long as Twin B is a girl." There was no room for negotiation. One of these babies had to be a girl.

At five months, I looked overdue and ready to pop with four months remaining. Additional ultrasounds indicated that Twin B was potentially a girl. The excitement of having boy-girl twins motivated me to clear out the after-season sales with matching boy-girl outfits.

Unexpected Issues

At six months, Dr. Kulbersh informed me that we might have a problem. Several ultrasounds were unable to detect a spine on Twin B.

"What does this mean?" I inquired.

"It may be nothing, spina bifida, or something else. I must send you to a specialist. If it's spina bifida, knowing will allow us to be prepared with the right kind of surgical delivery and a pediatric surgeon to repair the spine immediately, lessening the impact."

Our hopes and dreams hung in the "twilight zone." My husband and I tossed and turned all night. It seemed like an eternity waiting for that consultation. Days later, my husband held my hand as the specialist rolled that cold wand and jelly over my enormous belly.

"They are not conjoined!" She dictated to her nurse. "Please let Dr. Kulbersh know."

"Conjoined?" I inquired.

"I mean, the twins are not joined like Siamese twins," she clarified.

"I didn't know that was a possibility!"

"It was the first thing Dr. Kulbersh asked me to rule out. Now for the spine on Twin B," she explained.

After a careful examination, she said, "It appears Twin A is on top of Twin B, blocking sight of the spine every time an ultrasound is done. I think everything is fine. We can't be 100 percent sure, but my recommendation is for your doctor to proceed with a C-section and a pediatric surgeon on call. Twin A is definitely a boy. It appears that Twin B is a girl, but no guarantees."

God's Sovereign Plan

Hallelujah! The anxiety hovering over us had lifted. We drove home with tears of joy, gratitude, and contemplative thoughts.

"I think God is preparing me to have twin sons," I said. "I've been so concentrated on having a girl, I forgot what really matters is that they're both healthy."

After much introspection, I asked myself, "Who am I to determine the sex of my baby?" Only God knows the plans he has for us and our children. I realized I'd tried to play God. He was showing me he was sovereign and in control. Not me!

The Bible tells us that God knits us in our mother's womb. "You saw me before I was born. Every day of my life was recorded in your book. Every moment was laid out before a single day had passed" (Psalm 139:16).

At thirty-eight weeks, Dr. Kulbersh decided to take our twins by C-section. He was amazed I'd made it to thirty-eight weeks with no complications or labor.

On the morning of the surgery, my husband insisted on taking a profile picture of me. "You do look like the woman pregnant with twins in that picture." He chuckled. From the back, I looked normal. From the side, I looked like a balloon ready to pop.

Our thirty-eight-week emotional roller coaster became reality when I was rolled into the surgery room with two baby bassinets. "Honey, we're really having twins," I exclaimed. "And it doesn't matter what gender they are." Of course, I had one pink and one blue outfit to bring them home in.

The room was filled with laughter and anticipation.

The room was filled with laughter and anticipation. There were two delivery doctors, two pediatricians, two nurses, a gathering of medical students, and a pediatric surgeon on standby.

Within minutes, Dr. Plyler said, "Twin A is a boy, just like we thought." A few minutes later, He pulled Twin B from my womb. "Twin B is . . . another boy, and his spine is normal! No pediatric surgeon needed."

The weight of a heavy burden was lifted off our shoulders. Both babies were fine.

He held up Twin B for me to see front and back. "I'll take triplets if you can pull a girl out too." I giggled.

"That's it. Your twins weighed in at almost eight pounds each. You've just broken the record at this hospital," Dr. Plyler bragged. "If you want a daughter, you'll have to try again. Your risk of having twins again is high. You might end up with an all-male basketball team!"

God had spoken. In fact, the heavens were laughing.

God had spoken. In fact, the heavens were laughing. I tried to manipulate my cycle to get a daughter, and God gave me two sons! It was his will that we have three sons. We were blessed indeed. I now realize I was called to be a mother of three sons. My dreams of having a daughter were fulfilled when my sons chose their wives and my granddaughters were born. All good things happen in his timing. And my mom grabbed that cute little pink outfit and exchanged it for a matching blue one.

Boy-Raising Joys

Our lives were filled with sports, nature, and rough-and-tumble play. Whenever we voted on what to do as a family, I was always outnumbered. I learned to go with the flow. I knew the answer would always be biking, hiking, sports, and reptiles over shopping and tea parties. We taught our sons to appreciate God's creation. Exploring the great outdoors continues to be our favorite family pastime. We've vacationed in most of the national parks, creating memories we'll always treasure.

When our sons were school age, getting ready for school was easy. I put a warm, wet rag on each of their heads for a few minutes, then brushed their hair into place. I'm not sure I had the talent to fix a little girl's hair. God knew what he was doing when he gave me three boys.

However, I never liked reptiles.

No-Estrogen Zone

Years later, Alton and I traveled as guests of a national championship football team to one of their games. Before the game, we were eating with their coach and his wife. I never realized how much we had in common with this couple: three sons, our love for football, and breast cancer. She had lost her sister to breast cancer and was taking an estrogen blocker as prevention. In 2015, I had been diagnosed with breast cancer and was now taking an estrogen blocker to prevent my cancer from returning.

The husband looked at us and said, "Now there's no estrogen in our house."

My husband jokingly replied, "And there's no estrogen in our house either."

Both were right. Although I never thought my life and household would be lived estrogen-free, I learned to adjust and be grateful for good health and my three sons. God knew what he was doing.

GINNY DENT BRANT is a mother of three sons who grew up in Washington, DC. She has served as a counselor, wellness advocate, and adjunct professor. Her award-winning book, *Finding True Freedom: From the White House to the World*, was endorsed by Chuck Colson. *Unleash Your God-Given Healing: Eight Steps to Prevent and Survive Cancer* has won five awards. She speaks internationally and has been featured in media nationwide. Blog and more info at **ginnybrant.com**.

Stumbling, Fumbling Mom

Joni Topper

"DON'T PAY THE BILL." MY doctor spoke in his soft, kind voice. "You have plenty to take care of without paying my bill. If the office sends you one, ignore it."

Just a few months earlier, I'd left his office in tears. Tears of joy. The week after I filed for divorce from my husband, I discovered that I was pregnant. When my marriage dissolved in heartbreak and betrayal, one of my greatest regrets was the idea that my one-year-old daughter might be an only child. I grew up in a household with two sisters whose presence made life so sweet. I could not imagine my precious daughter growing up without a sister of her own.

Even though the pregnancy was unexpected, it felt like an answered prayer. No one understood my joy except God. How could I be happy about entering single life at twenty-three years old with a toddler and being pregnant at the same time? It made no sense from the outside looking in.

Another Cesarean Delivery

My dad stood by my side as the nurse gave me a shot I needed in preparation for a cesarean delivery. I cried, but no tears came to my eyes. My poor Dad did not know what to say to me, but he longed to offer me comfort. The strange sensation of having no tears matched what I'd been feeling for months. Nothing seemed natural, but a deep calm ran inside me.

Later, I woke up in the recovery room to the sound of my doctor's voice.

"Look, he's peeing all over the room. It's a boy." He held a Polaroid picture up for me to see. His words rang in my head. "A boy?" I had two sisters. Our first round of babies were all girls. My mom had two sisters. They all had girls. My family did not know what to do with boys.

After my first cesarean, I'd gotten a womb infection and been sick for weeks. This was a very different experience. The day I left the hospital, I went home and dressed my two beautiful children in cute outfits and went to the mall to exchange all the pink baby clothes for blue. Midway through my shopping experience, my energy bottomed out. I sat in the corridor and recovered my stamina enough to get back home. Ready to blast into my new life with energy, my stumbling body needed a little recovery time.

Stressful First Checkup

At the two-week checkup for my baby boy, the nurse had to prick his heel numerous times to get a blood sample. Rodney screamed incessantly from that, which meant the doctor had to put his professional skills into action to get a long enough pause to listen to his heart. Next, he checked to see if his circumcision healed properly. No one had instructed me at the hospital when the procedure occurred that I should keep the skin stretched, or it might grow back. I had not tended to it correctly, and the doctor's attention to the matter made Rodney scream even more.

By the time his exam ended, my nerves were shattered. "Do you have anything to calm the mother?" I asked the doctor. He'd waited till the baby settled, then came in to assure me that if I ever needed help, his staff would answer the call.

"Do you have anything to calm the mother?" I asked the doctor.

"Don't let yourself get to a point of despair. Let someone help you." He did not know that my family and church family were a strong support system. His calm, nonjudgmental words expressed compassion for me as a young mother. Though I never called, the offer meant a lot.

Return to Church

During my pregnancy, I'd sat out of church and watched a weekly broadcast of a TV preacher. It was the only season of my life that I had not been in church, but I did not want to go to my couples' class while in the middle of a divorce, and I did not want to go to the singles' class pregnant.

When Rodney was ten days old, I went back to church. That day I met Ernest, who would later become my husband.

Most of our courtship centered around things at church. I did not have the freedom or desire to ditch my babies and go looking for a man. I was not looking for a replacement husband. My "wasband" did not remain in my life or the kids' lives.

One of my first dates with Ernest included taking my baby to dinner with us. He was a beautiful child and easy to care for. He slept well and traveled well. I could go anywhere with him because his big brown eyes took in everything with little sign of emotion. In fact, I almost worried about him because he was so even-tempered. He did not laugh or cry much. He was just there.

Then that night in the restaurant, he woke up and screamed the entire time we were out. Much to my surprise, my date did not drop us off and head for the hills. He helped me change diapers and tend to the baby's needs.

Rodney never slowed down after that. He was like a racehorse out of the gate. He possessed no gear but high gear, clearly growing into a person that *happened* to you.

New Last Name

After Ernest and I married, he adopted my children. On adoption day, his mother made the kids t-shirts with their new last name and baked us a cake decorated with a pot of gold at the end of a rainbow. I bought Ernest bubble gum cigars to hand out, pink ones for his new daughter and blue ones for his new son.

Soon after blending our family, we moved to the Texas Hill Country and bought land. We cleared brush and cedar, preparing a place to build a home. Four-year-old Rodney found a machete and acted as if he'd discovered the perfect tool. He clearly wanted to help. We stood side by side with our hands on our hips, searching for a project. I hoped to occupy him and keep him away from his sister with that blade. Noticing a tree stump about a foot in diameter that stood about four feet tall after we'd taken the top off, I said, "Go cut that one down. It's still too tall."

Four-year-old Rodney found a machete and acted as if he'd discovered the perfect tool.

I sent him toward the stump, which was in my clear view yet far enough removed that no one else would get in his way. He swung that machete at the stump for days, chipping away at the hard wood as if he were a grown-up contributor to the backwoods country life we were carving out of this piece of untouched land.

Looking back, I realize that giving a four-year-old a machete is more akin to a bumbling parental choice than a wise one, but I still attribute his upper body strength and coordination to that exercise. I am thankful that he did not injure himself in the process.

No Dull Moments

While we built, we set up a port-a-potty on the front porch of the house. Located three miles down a dirt road, we were separated enough from our neighbors that no one could see us. One day Rodney used the potty, and as he flushed, the chemicals splashed back into his face. Immediately, he grabbed his eyes, screaming.

We did not have running water yet, but our neighbor, located about 300 yards away, had an outdoor shower. I acted quickly, grabbing

Rodney and running to the shower. I called for my neighbor and started washing the boy's eyes and face. Fortunately, the neighbor was home. While I continued flushing Rodney's eyes, she called 911 for me and asked where we should go for medical attention.

I grabbed the container that held the chemicals, and we rushed to the nearest ER.

I grabbed the container that held the chemicals, and we rushed to the nearest ER, about forty-five minutes away, praying the whole time. Fortunately, his eyes only had mild abrasions. The doctor said that different chemicals would have damaged his eyes permanently, and there would have been nothing we could do regardless of how fast we acted. Once again, a crisis averted.

However, it wouldn't be the last. My husband drank a lot of tea, so we often took a gallon water bottle full of tea with us to our work site. It usually sat on the tailgate of the truck. We used a chainsaw for some of our projects, and a chainsaw uses fuel with oil added. It is nearly the same color as tea. You know where this is going here, don't you?

One day, Rodney picked up the gallon jug of chainsaw fuel and took a big swig of it, thinking he had grabbed the tea. We'd been told that if you ingested gasoline, you could swallow raw eggs to induce vomiting. We had chickens, so we cracked a few eggs, and Rodney drank them. Nothing. He said he liked the way they tasted.

Fortunately, we later learned that the fuel burns the esophagus going down, so having it come back up is not a good idea anyway. Oh, the things we learned that we never have wanted to know.

An Inquiring Mind

Four-year-old Rodney once surprised a handsome young worker in a western store with a question while we shopped. He stared at the salesman with his big brown eyes, then asked, "Are you my dad?"

The kind young man glanced at me. I wanted to melt into the wallpaper. Rodney's biological dad's parents remained a constant in his life, so he knew his other "dad" existed, but he did not know him. Maybe the youngster confused you "*have* not because you ask not" with "you *know* not because you ask not." In any case, I shuffled right on out of that store.

When Ernest and I married, I'd asked him what he wanted the kids to call him. "I don't care. They can call me anything they are comfortable with. I'm going to love them the same no matter what."

As a mom, I could not have hoped for any better answer. Both kids call him Dad, and that's what he's been in every sense of the word.

Some of the things we do right as parents come naturally, some of them we learn, and some of them we stumble into by the grace of God. I've been a protected, stumbling, fumbling mom since day one. Motherhood usually does not frighten me because I know God loves my children even more than I do. He also knew what he was doing when he allowed me the joy of parenting my oh-so-full-of-life little boy.

JONI TOPPER radiates God's glory by sharing everyday moments in riveting storyteller fashion—the inspiration for Joni's Morning Glory Ministry. Whether wearing her grandmother, author, or speaker hat, Joni's favorite description of herself is, "One who desires to look like Jesus." As a singer/songwriter, she emanates joy. Joni and her husband, Ernest, have been married for over forty-one years. Check out her blog at **Morninggloryministry.com**.

Building Faith—From What-Ifs to What Is

Melissa Meyer

I HELD MY BREATH AS MY son, Bennett, stood on tiptoes, tongue poking out the side of his mouth in concentration. He reached up over his head to place another toy block on the tower—a stack of single blocks on top of one another. It swayed ever so slightly as he placed another one. As he released the block and moved his chubby preschool hand away, the tall stack came crashing down, making a loud noise as the wooden squares met the kitchen floor.

We laughed at the crash, and then I said, "Okay, why don't you build another tower? But now, instead of stacking it all up on one block, use several blocks at the bottom."

As he nodded in agreement, his shaggy red hair bounced up and down on his forehead. He started with four blocks, side by side, then three blocks, then two, then he continued adding to the height by stacking one on top of another.

This time, he needed to get the step stool from the bathroom. The one he used to wash his hands at the sink. It was the only way he could reach the top of his tower. The stack still crashed to the floor, making an even louder noise because of the added blocks. We laughed again.

But Bennett's second tower had stood longer and was taller than the first because it had a better foundation. And the foundation was still intact when the figurative dust had settled.

A Thwarted Plan

"Be careful," I warned as my husband and our two kids stepped out of our van. "The parking lot and sidewalk are slippery. Don't fall and hurt yourself."

Little did I know what the day would bring. My verbal warning should've been my first clue to get back in the van immediately and drive home.

Little did I know what the day would bring.

It was a frigid January day in 2021. Our Wisconsin winters are long, but we hearty northerners know how to make the most out of the, at times, seemingly never-ending season.

This day found us at the local park near our home. Even though our kids were seven and four years old and had lived their entire lives in Wisconsin, they had never been sledding before. I know. I heard you gasp as you read that.

With sleds in hand, my husband and the kids started trudging up the giant hill. A popular sledding spot in town, it was busy at the park but not crowded. We had decided that I would stay put to greet our first-time sledders with cheers and giggles when they got to the bottom.

A big playground sat at the bottom of the hill, and the city had put up a long, orange, plastic snow fence to keep any sledders from hitting the playground equipment. Usually, anyone on a sled wouldn't have enough speed to reach the snow fence. However, because steel posts anchored the snow fence, they'd also placed a hay bale in front of each post to serve as a buffer on the chance a super-speedy sledder got that far.

It hadn't snowed for a few days. The hill had a bit of a sheen to it from snow slowly morphing into ice as sledders had packed it down over the past couple of days. My mother's intuition tingled slightly at the sight of the shiny snow, but I ignored the faint din of an internal alarm bell.

The plan was for our daughter to go down solo, and my husband would sit on the sled with our son. Except I guess no one told Bennett the plan. I was chatting with a neighbor, so I had taken my eyes off my family as they worked their way up the hill. Suddenly, I saw Bennett rocketing down on his sled—alone. He had decided to just sit on his sled and go as his dad and sister trudged ahead.

A Shaken Foundation

Even though he didn't start at the top of the hill, he was going way too fast. The look of terror on his face made me sprint toward him, screaming at him to roll off. Of course, he couldn't hear me because I was too far away. And even if he had heard my instructions, he didn't know how to pitch himself off a speeding sled.

I hurried toward him and watched in horror as he made high-speed impact with the only pole without a hay bale in front of it. The bale had slid to the side, leaving the five-inch-wide pole exposed in this vast park. What were the chances of it injuring someone? A 100 percent chance on this day.

Bennett hurtled forward, hitting the pole face-first as his sled came to an abrupt stop. I screamed his name. He wasn't moving as I approached. All I could think about was a family from my hometown who had lost a young daughter in a tragic sledding accident when she hit a wooden fence post.

I fell to my knees beside him, relieved he wasn't unconscious but wailing instead.

I laid him back and told him I was right there. I have zero medical training. But I've watched enough medical dramas that I knew not to move his neck. I whipped off his boots and asked him to wiggle his toes. He could wiggle his toes. More relief. But still, plenty of panic spewed out of my heart! By now, my neighbor had caught up to me, and I cried out to her, "I don't know what to do!"

I screamed my husband's name. He was so far up the hill that he had no idea what had happened. I listened to the squeals and screams of delight from my daughter and husband coming down the hill as it mingled with my son's howling in fear and pain.

After my husband arrived on the scene, he carried Bennett to the van. We placed him in his car seat and headed to the ER. My first tears finally came during the three-mile drive. I had never felt such fear as I did in those moments.

When I had to tell the ER staff what had happened, I cried again and couldn't stop. I felt horrible as a mother. I let my baby get hurt. On my watch.

After a CT scan, an ultrasound on a neck artery, and a bandaged-up face, we left the ER with Bennett feeling more like himself again. He didn't even need stitches. He looked like he had a road rash on his face and neck.

My injured little guy wanted to stick close to me. So, he slept in a nest of blankets right next to my bed. The following morning, Bennett was hungry and very peppy. I couldn't believe how fast he was bouncing back.

A Long Recovery—For Me

My son's neck and face recovered faster than my aching heart. The swelling went down the next day, and four days later, we could hardly tell he had been injured.

However, I struggled for weeks. Every time I would replay the events in my mind or thought about the what-ifs, I would get teary-eyed. *How could I have let that happen? Why didn't I trust my intuition when I had an uneasy feeling upon arrival at the park? What kind of mother lets her kid slide down a giant, icy hill on his inaugural run? What if something much worse had happened?*

It didn't matter to me if it was "just one of those things" or that I didn't know what was going to happen. Or even that Bennett was the third sledding accident in the local ER *that day*.

I talked to God a lot in the days following the accident. I thanked him for protecting Bennett. But mostly, I told God all about my struggle with guilt. I asked him to take the burden away. I pictured myself laying the load at the foot of the cross. I read and reread Jesus's words, "Come to me, all of you who are weary and carry heavy burdens, and I will give you rest. Take my yoke upon you. Let me teach you, because I am humble and gentle at heart, and you will find rest for your souls" (Matthew 11:28–29).

And even though I've been walking with Jesus in a relationship for many years, I couldn't get past self-blame. I did all the things I knew should help, such as praying and meditating on Scripture. I did what had gotten me through tough times before. But the guilt would not relent.

I reached out to a few close Christian girlfriends, told them what had happened . . . I asked for help.

Finally, I called in the troops. My husband and I hadn't shared with too many people what had happened. Just a few family members. But I needed support. I reached out to a few close Christian girlfriends, told them what had happened and how guilty I felt. I asked for help. And my troops rallied by lifting me up in prayer. Within two days, I was feeling so much lighter and free from guilt. It felt as though my feet were once again planted on the firm foundation of God's faithfulness and his promises.

Sometimes, when your confidence in yourself as a boy mom has tumbled to the ground like a tower of toy blocks, you need your friends to come alongside you to help you remember your firm foundation built on God.

A Renewed Trust

It's hard being a boy mom. There are times when they're going to get hurt. There are times when their decisions are going to scare you.

There are plenty of times that you're going to doubt your abilities as a mom. There are times when you may feel as if God is far away.

But just know, mama, that God loves you, and he loves your son. More than you do, even though that may seem impossible.

Our feelings come and go. They aren't trustworthy because they often depend on the present situation. Our feelings can make us feel as if we're on shaky ground that won't hold fast. But feelings are temporary. The love and character of God are forever. His promises will never fail. He is our foundation that will never crumble, especially after the figurative dust has settled.

MELISSA MEYER is a freelance writer for small businesses and entrepreneurs. Her business name, Bets & Ben Creative, is named after her children, Betsy and Bennett. She and her husband, Chip, live in Hudson, WI, with their children and two naughty kitties, Buddy and Oliver. When she's not writing for clients, you might find her avoiding housework by reading a novel, listening to a podcast, or enjoying "afternoon coffee" like a good Scandinavian should. **betsandbencreative.com**

Bubble Wrap, Broken Bones, and Blessings

Michelle Rayburn

PHIL AND I HAD JUST returned from a dinner for two and were filling the private whirlpool in our suite when I noticed the red message light blinking on the hotel's bedside phone. *Hmm. I wonder what I forgot to pack.*

Mere hours had passed since we'd dropped off the boys at my parents' house, left instructions and emergency contact numbers (no cell phones in those days), kissed their sweet cheeks, and skipped town for the weekend. Our first getaway for the two of us since our second son's birth about six months earlier.

I dialed the front desk to retrieve the message. My brother's voice. "Call home as soon as possible," Brett said. *Why is he the one calling?*

My heart sank. My mom would have called. *It must be terrible news.* And the kids should have been in bed by now.

Brett answered the phone at the farm. He didn't waste time on small talk. "Now, don't come home, but . . ."

That registered high on my mom meter. Nothing good would come from anything that started with "Don't come home, but . . ."

"Dallas broke his arm, and he's at the ER with Mom and Dad. But Mom doesn't want you to come home. She says everything will be fine." I learned my two siblings were home with our infant, who was tucked into bed for the night, while my parents drove the thirty minutes to the hospital.

"How did he do that?" I asked, imagining they had allowed him to climb the silo or jump from the haymow or something I'd equally disapprove of.

"He jumped off the recliner footrest."

"Jumped, as in from only two feet above the floor? Are you certain it's broken?"

Really, I do trust my parents, but I was struggling to hold back the overreactive gremlin that squirmed inside of me. *Thank goodness I thought to include an emergency consent form, the doctor's name, medical history numbers, and insurance info in the diaper bag. Oh, man, I forgot the bubble wrap!*

He assured me that the arm was indeed broken—both bones clean through—as indicated by the severe bend in the forearm that prompted the trip to the ER. After all, Grandma, the nurse, ought to know.

Details

I had to ask my sister, Becki, to fill in the details as I was working on this story. First, she was *there*. But also, she's younger and still has her premenopausal brain, which is much better at details than mine.

Becki was in the "hazardous" chair, and Dallas, dressed in his pajamas, was having a little play time before bed. As she described it, this all sounded much safer than the usual shenanigans that my husband regularly did with the boys before bed.

"He would climb up the recliner and give me a kiss and then jump off," she said. He did it a few times, and then after that fateful jump, "he stood up and looked at me, holding up his arm," she said. How she described the dip in the middle of his forearm still gives me the heebie-jeebies.

> This all sounded much safer than the usual shenanigans that my husband regularly did with the boys before bed.

Grandma had thought to take his favorite stuffed Barney along when they bundled Dallas up for the drive.

My mom said they'd pressed the little button in the toy's hand, singing the Barney theme song together over and over, she and my sedated two-year-old. "I love you. You love . . ."

He chose purple for his cast, of course—Barney purple. Or at least the closest thing to Barney purple that an ER had in stock.

I won't forget my dad describing the distress to his grandpa heart when listening in on the reduction, a procedure to manipulate and realign the broken bones without cutting the skin open. Picturing it invaded my imagination too. Ugh.

For this, the medical team administers an IV similar to what a surgeon might use for removing wisdom teeth. Conscious sedation means the patient might cry out during the procedure but won't remember any pain. But that doesn't mean the adults on the other side of the curtain or out in the hallway don't feel every cry and whimper to the core. (Now that I'm a grandma, I understand this ache. I cried when a grandchild broke away from my grasp and lurched toward the coffee table. Felt every cry. Felt totally responsible for the wound on her brow.)

Decisions

These are the moments when parents wrestle with decisions that have no perfect solutions. Do we stay? Do we go home? Is there anything different we can do that isn't already being done? Am I a bad mother for not running to his side? Will he remember the trauma later?

We decided to do what anyone torn by a tough decision does: postpone it. By this time, it was past everyone's bedtimes—adults included. We would see how Dallas was in the morning and then determine what to do. Besides, I wasn't going to decide until I'd had my free breakfast at Denny's.

We didn't have texting or video chats. We didn't have cell phones. No one could send a photo to prove all was well. We had prepaid cards from AT&T and punched a loooong pin number into a telephone to place a call. Get one number wrong and you had to start over. Helicopter parenting is much more difficult with limited communication. You don't know what you don't know.

I called home in the morning.

My mom answered with her usual phone cheerfulness. "He's up and playing. He slept in my bed last night so I could monitor him. He's a little pale and tired but otherwise doing fine." He didn't seem much bothered by the ordeal.

One of the most difficult moments of my parenting years was deciding to stay put in that hotel room for those two nights while I knew one of my babies was back home in a purple cast.

Many mothers might have rushed home. In my defense, in case you'd have handled it differently, I was mom-weary. Six months of enduring colicky wailing from an infant really messes with your brain. I'll save that story for another time. I desperately craved uninterrupted time with Phil.

Nurse Grandma had this. This wasn't a teenage babysitter. My mom had raised three children, *and* she was a licensed nurse. So, why was this such a struggle?

You're a good mom, whatever you decide.
We each do our own thing.

Moms, you know the inner turmoil of wanting to do two things simultaneously. These are the situations that turn our hair gray and lead to adrenal fatigue. We want to rescue our sons and kiss away their pain, but we want to raise independent boys who eventually become self-sufficient men. Yet, we also want to make sure others perceive us as good moms in that process, right?

In case you have your own similar battles in your heart and mind, this is for you: you're a good mom, whatever you decide. We each do our own thing.

Detours

I didn't start out as a parent who thought a little dirt on the pacifier was an immune booster or a bump on the noggin was as harmless as a kiss. We sanitized everything everywhere all the time. I made sure they avoided all things remotely hazardous. It isn't that I hovered, but—okay, I did hover. Isn't that the obligation of new parents?

However, the decision to stay put on our couple's getaway was a start in veering off the overprotective path. That weekend, I learned that I couldn't protect my sons from all harm and that I can't always be the one to fix things. I initially launched into worry and started thinking of everything this disruption would affect. It was Dallas's dominant arm. He was in the beginning of potty training and definitely not ready to get a pull-up off with one arm. *Will he still be left-handed after months in a cast?* I wondered. Spoiler alert: he was!

We were in the early stages of considering a job change, which would also affect our health insurance—and the follow-up appointments. *Will our new insurance cover a preexisting condition? Does COBRA cover it in between now and the new insurance?*

I'm a fixer and a planner. But I couldn't fix or plan my way out of this. I had to trust that God—and Grandpa and Grandma—could handle this for two days. When I set aside the worries and desire to arrange all the details, God showed me that when I put our boys in his hands, he already had others ready to work things out. My parents and young-adult siblings managed beautifully!

It wouldn't be the last time I'd have to trust God to work things out. Whether it was dropping one off at camp or applying for a passport and prepping another for a mission trip to South America, each situation offered more practice for trusting God. One day, I'd hand over the Jeep keys to a teen with a freshly minted license and watch two boys drive off to school. Another day, I'd get a call in the middle of teaching piano lessons: "Mom, don't panic."

Why do they start calls this way?

"I just wiped out my motorcycle, and I'm pretty sure I need stitches. Can you come get me?"

Like the psalmist, I can say, "My help comes from the LORD, who made heaven and earth! (Psalm 121:1). As he did with the Israelite pilgrims, the Lord watches over my sons and never sleeps. He stands beside them. "The LORD keeps watch over you as you come and go, both now and forever" (v. 8).

Mom friends, God watches over us too. Even when worry crops up and we're battling something beyond our control, he is beside us and our little boys—and big boys—watching with love. Take heart. And take a deep breath. He's got this.

MICHELLE RAYBURN is an author and podcast host who helps others find hope in the trashy stuff of life. She has an MA in ministry leadership and writes Christian living books, humor, and Bible studies. Together with her husband, they've raised two sons and gained two daughters-in-law—plus three granddaughters (go estrogen team!) and a grandson. Dark chocolate, an iced coffee, and a good book in the hammock top Michelle's favorites list. **michellerayburn.com**

Wearing the Dad Hat—Or Face

Valerie McNulty

I DON'T THINK I CAN KEEP *up this pace. Exhausted is an understatement.* These thoughts consistently ran through my mind during my husband's last deployment. You know what people say: "Raising boys is not for the faint of heart." Well, add the military lifestyle into the mix, and you have one crazy, chaotic life. This lifestyle is challenging, and while I try to roll with the punches, more often than not, I feel like a failure. Even my best efforts seem to fall short, and I second-guess my abilities as a wife and mother.

On the flip side, raising boys in this military lifestyle is also incredibly beautiful. My boys have such a love and gratitude for this country that just radiates out of them. To watch them be so proud of their dad and consistently cheer him on through the sacrifices means the world.

Multiple Hats Is Hard Work

Due to our lifestyle, I often have to wear multiple hats. I regularly wear my wife and mom hats and wear the dad hat more frequently than I would prefer. Now, I can do a lot of things, and I can wear a lot of hats, but that is a hat that will never quite fit. I can even go as far as saying the same things my husband would typically say or using the same tone of voice or discipline style and still not measure up to the real thing. My boys are fully aware of this fact too. It's what makes solo parenting for extended amounts of time challenging.

> No amount of Facetime calls, no bribes or distractions will take away from the fact that my sons miss their father.

There is nothing that can replace their daddy. No amount of Facetime calls, no bribes or distractions will take away from the fact that my sons miss their father. They miss wrestling with him the moment he walks in the door. They miss his dad jokes that make them endlessly laugh. They miss the bedtime pow-wows and prayers at night. My boys feel the void of their daddy being absent. Despite my best efforts of trying to wear the dad hat, something I have learned is that community is necessary.

Raising Children Takes a Village

During our almost five years of living at Fort Carson, Colorado, my husband was away most of that time. With a nine-month deployment followed by an eleven-month deployment, field training exercises, various temporary duty travel (TDY) assignments, and whatever else the Army wanted to tack on, it's safe to say my husband's head was hardly on his pillow in our home. Due to this, I had to learn how to not only ask for help but be okay with accepting it. I had to learn firsthand the meaning of the saying "It takes a village."

Living on a military installation is similar to being transported back in time. Picture the 1950s when everyone does life in their front yards. Heaven forbid you take your dog on a quick walk because that will cost you an extra hour. Everyone knows and speaks with one another, and privacy goes out the window. To some, this sounds atrocious, but I have found it to be beautiful and vital to my survival.

I can't tell you how many times I've opened my front door to a friendly face of someone holding out a cup of coffee, or when sickness would wipe me and my boys out, my neighbors would spring into action. These people from all walks of life embody the hands and feet of Jesus. I will always be amazed at the compassion I have experienced due to the military lifestyle.

It was no secret that I was riding the struggle bus. I didn't even have to say anything. I'm assuming my face said it all. The deployment that initially was only going to last four months was now well into the ninth month. Both boys were feeling the repercussions of the lengthy deployment as well. My oldest had many questions and was confused why just his dad needed to be gone. My youngest couldn't articulate his feelings, leading to full-blown meltdowns at the flip of a switch.

If there was an end to my rope, I was at it. Between the big emotions, tantrums, and never-ending questions, I felt as if I was in a never-ending season, and every day was the same. I prayed for God to speed up time. I tried to rely on him because my strength was not cutting it anymore. I'm sure you can guess it, but God did not speed up time. In fact, he lengthened it. He's funny like that.

When I reflect on this particular season and reminisce on the exhaustion from parenting two boys alone for eleven months, I find comfort in knowing God was with me every step. He provided friends who encouraged me and helped me when I couldn't do one more thing. This village of mine didn't ask if I needed help; they just insisted. They would come over with meals. They would fold the mountain of laundry on my couch. They would hold and rock my screaming toddler to give me a break.

I had to learn to set my pride aside and allow others the opportunity to help. Being vulnerable and allowing someone into the mess opens the door to a deeper relationship, where raw emotion with brutal honesty is welcome. Somehow, even in our darkest moments, we can experience love, joy, and laughter.

Laughter Is the Best Medicine

Receiving packages during that time was a regular occurrence in our household. The mailman knew our house well, whether it was a care package from our home church in Georgia, thinking-of-you gifts from grandparents, or the multitude of items I purchased on Amazon amid my sadness. One day, we received a package with my husband's name on the return address. My face lit up. He took the time to send us a package. My boys immediately came running to the door.

"Mommy, is that for me?"

"Can we open it?"

Without hesitation, I said, "Absolutely," and the boys tore into the big box. Suddenly, a shriek of laughter filled the room. At that moment, my oldest pulled a giant pillow out of the box with my husband's smiling face on it.

I looked in the box for anything else, and lying on the bottom was a small note that said, "Hey, pretty lady, I know my absence has been hard, and it feels like it's never going to end. I hope that this pillow of my face makes you smile."

The boys and I looked at the oversized pillow again and burst into laughter. This moment was the medicine that my soul needed. My sons and I took turns passing around the pillow and pretending to be Daddy.

My sons and I took turns passing around the pillow and pretending to be Daddy.

To see my oldest spit out dad jokes as if they were going out of style while holding my husband's face in front of his is a memory I will always cherish. Although my husband bought the gift for me, I think it meant even more to my boys. My youngest would light up whenever I put the pillow in front of my face. Something as simple as a pillow made the world's weight disappear off my shoulders and filled my heart with joy.

That evening was the highlight of the entire deployment. I may not be able to wear the dad hat very well, but that night I tried my best. I chased my boys around the living room with the pillow in front of my face. Endless squeals and laughter filled the air. We placed my husband's face on his side of the bed and put another pillow under the covers. It looked as if my husband were present and lying in bed. I let them jump on the bed around that pillow and pretend they were wrestling with their father. This thoughtful gift and the joy it brought all of us filled my cup to the brim.

We Need a Father

Although time trucked on and didn't seem to move fast enough, I learned a valuable lesson through my boys during that deployment. My heart hurt as they navigated their emotions of saying goodbye to their hero when he'd left. I watched them miss their father. I saw how they yearned for him and cherished their time together, even if it was on a Facetime call. I tried to find ways to help alleviate the aching in their little hearts.

My sons were fortunate to have some incredible male role models in their life during this time, but not one could replace their daddy. As I think of their need for their father, it reminds me of my need for a Father, not the earthly kind.

I am so thankful for my heavenly Father, who sees me as I am. When I am weak, he is strong. When I feel afraid or anxious, he comforts me. Nothing can take his place. There is absolutely nothing that measures up. In a season where I felt as if I couldn't go another step, he wrapped my boys and me up in his loving arms, so I felt peace in his presence even during the most challenging moments. He walked alongside me and said, "Valerie, fear not, for I am with you. I will not leave you or forsake you."

VALERIE MCNULTY is a military wife, mother of two boys, and author. She is a content writer and the assistant content director for Homefront Heroes Ministries. If Valerie is not dreaming up new book ideas, you can find her enjoying outdoor adventures with her family. If you would like to connect with Valerie, you can follow her on Facebook @ValerieMcNultyAuthor or on her website at **valeriemcnulty.com**.

Growing Boys

From Foster to Forever

Betty Predmore

HE WALKED INTO MY HOUSE the day after his sixth birthday. The moment he entered, I became a foster mom. I had no idea how this would go, but I had agreed to foster him, his little brother, and his baby sister, and I was going to give it my best shot.

This little guy was skinny and shy. He had been moved to several different homes in his three years of foster care, and some of them had not been the most pleasant experience for a child. Because of this, he seemed both apprehensive about his new surroundings and comfortable with walking into a strange home.

A Boy Needing Reassurance

On my second day of caring for him, I had to take him for dental surgery, which required a two-hour trip to and from the hospital, giving us time to get acquainted. It was then, in the car, that he called me "Mom" for the first time, and my heart melted.

The first two weeks were tough for him. He was unsure about the situation, hopeful yet doubting at the same time. Every time I placed a meal in front of him, he said to me, "Mom, will we eat again today?" I reassured him that he would indeed have three meals each day, along with snacks.

Whenever we left the house to go anywhere, his question was, "Mom, am I coming back here?"

My reply was, "Yes, Bryan, we will be back in just a little while."

After a couple of weeks, his trust in me was secure, and he stopped asking those questions. Day by day, he became a comfortable, rambunctious little kindergartener with a ready smile and a sweet hug.

Several months into their stay, an occasion arose where I couldn't take the children to the monthly visitation that was scheduled with an elderly family member. I had faithfully taken them to that appointment every month and waited in my car while they spent an hour with her. But on this day, I simply could not get them there.

I called the social worker, who then told me she would have a driver pick them up for the visit and bring them home afterward. When the driver showed up, he loaded them into his van. Bryan stared straight at me the whole time with a look that said he was certain he was never coming back to our house again. I understood that in his mind, his worse fears were being answered, and he was being moved to another house.

My heart broke for him as I watched them drive away with his eyes on me as if it were the last time he would see me. His stare spoke the words he didn't say out loud, "I knew it!"

My heart broke for him as I watched them drive away with his eyes on me.

That was the longest hour of my life. I couldn't wait to get them back. I wanted Bryan to see that he was coming back to our home and that we were not abandoning him. I don't know which one of us was more relieved when that van pulled into our driveway, but I can assure you it was a happy reunion.

A Boy Needing a Family

Bryan and his siblings molded themselves into our already-bountiful family, and each gained their own sweet relationships with their new siblings. Words will never express the way it touched my heart to see my biological children love and nurture these new children so openly and willingly.

Each one of them had a particular older sibling that they were especially close to. This gave them a sense of family with all the kids but also a special relationship with one where they could feel even more special.

Siblings have a special relationship, and to see mine lovingly adapt three new little people into the relationship they'd nurtured over many years was a gift from God that I will never forget. I am eternally proud of them for their love, grace, compassion, and acceptance.

A Boy Needing Permanence

That first year was filled with visits from social workers, trips to the hospital for a health condition, and as much fun as we could pack in. We camped in the mountains, went to a water park, went boating and tubing, took bike rides, enjoyed family movie nights, and so much more.

Then came the social worker's words that made my heart stop. "These kids are being placed for adoption." What did this mean for us? Would they take these precious children from our home? I was terrified. I asked for more information, and the social worker clarified the facts and offered us the opportunity to apply for adoption.

All day, I worried as I waited for my husband to get home. Would he want to adopt? He had already taken on my four biological children, so would he be willing to take on more? We had discussed fostering but never adoption.

I tried to imagine telling Bryan that he would not be coming back to our home. I couldn't fathom doing that to this shy little boy who had warmed up to us so well. All the trust we had built would be broken, and all his insecurities would rise back to the surface.

So, I paced, and I waited, and I prayed. When my husband came home from work, I told him what the social worker had said. I will never forget the relief I felt when he looked at me and said, "Well, we'd better get that paperwork done." And thus began the process of making three little children a permanent part of our beautiful chaos.

The Bible says, "Pure and genuine religion in the sight of God the Father means caring for orphans and widows in their distress and refusing to let the world corrupt you" (James 1:27). While we might have been practicing that genuine religion by offering a home to these children, it was us who received the greatest blessing.

Adoption day was a beautiful day. We had family join us at the courthouse when a very special judge came in on his day off to make our family whole. Two little boys in suits and a little girl in a beautiful dress became the youngest of our tribe, and it was definitely a day to celebrate.

Bryan got to change his last name at school and learn to spell Predmore. He got to pick his own middle name, and he chose my maiden name. I believe it was then that he truly felt safe from being removed from us.

A Boy Needing Jesus

One of the greatest blessings was taking the kids to our church and teaching them about Jesus. They learned the stories of the Bible and how to pray for our family and others. They learned the songs that have been passed down to children through the ages, and they learned what it means to be a part of a church family.

Later, they would learn the blessing of being a part of a youth group and what it really means to serve God. Bryan and his younger siblings would spend hours serving the homeless and giving to the needy in the community. That is how we live, and they fit right into that.

It is a true comfort to me to know that my children know Jesus and he is their comfort and source of strength. That is my most important job, along with ensuring they know how much they are loved.

A Family Needing a Boy

One of the things I find most different between raising boys and raising girls is that boys tend to be less demonstrative with their affections, typically. Bryan does not fit that mold at all. He has always been the initiator of hugs and the speaker of "I love you." As he has grown and become a young adult, he has shown responsibility and maturity that many twice his age don't possess. He is still quick with a hug, never shy about saying "I love you," and always willing to help.

> This young man blesses my heart even more than that little boy did so many years ago.

That shy little six-year-old is still a bit on the shy side. He is quieter than most of his siblings. He sits back and observes. He lives just down the street from me now, and many mornings I come down my stairs to see him waiting to have coffee with me. This young man blesses my heart even more than that little boy did so many years ago.

I thank God for the privilege of raising Bryan. I praise him for the trust he put into our family to bring this boy up the way we should. We had no idea adoption would ever be a part of our lives. Now we often must be reminded that we adopted. To us, these kids are just ours. We didn't realize our family was incomplete until they walked in our door. Now we are the family God intended us to be.

Sharing the gospel through writing and speaking is one of **BETTY PREDMORE's** favorite things to do. She engages her audiences with her easy, conversational style. Her words make women pause and ponder the possibilities of a beautiful life with Christ. As an author, Christian communicator and ministry leader, Betty uses every opportunity to encourage women to live their best life in Christ and overcome the strongholds that hold them captive. You can visit Betty at **momsenseinc.org.**

You've Been Drafted

Stacy Sanchez

"INCOMING!"

Incoming? What does that mean? As I climbed the stairs carrying a basket piled high with laundry, I was about to discover exactly what it meant. It meant I had better run FAST because World War III had just broken out in my hallway. I was now caught in the middle of a stomp rocket war.

Dodging flying bullets, I bobbed and weaved like a wide receiver—with an outstretched arm, knocking whatever or whoever out of my way. Who cared about those newly folded towels anymore? While I ran the gauntlet between enemy positions, they got tossed so the basket could become a shield to protect my face.

The screams of "Give up! You're dead meat!" "No, you are!" were deafening.

"Fire in the hole!" came from the oldest.

Girl, you better tuck and roll. Better yet, dive and take cover! Protect the new lashes! Those babies cost you a fortune.

More bullets ripped across my brow. One bounced off my leg. The next my arm. The last hit the side of my neck, and now I'm seriously over it.

"Hey! Ouch! Enough! I didn't enlist in the army. I don't want to be a casualty of war."

If you are the mother of elementary school aged boys, welcome to the army. You've been drafted.

Noise With Dirt on 'Em

Raising boys is not for the faint of heart. It takes a strong mother who can dodge Nerf bullets one minute and tenderly kiss boo-boos the next. Elementary school age boys are a combination of sweat, energy, curiosity, and spunk. No sooner have you mopped the floor than they are following behind you with an "invention" made from something out of the garbage can, your hairbrush, and super glue. Breathe deep and pick your battles. The floor can wait. What's glued to his forehead cannot.

When I was raising my three boys, I would complain to my grandmother about their mess and noise. She had a listening ear and wisdom one can only obtain from raising a boy herself.

"I'm so over this, Grandma! I'll clean something, and two minutes later, it's dirty again. I give up! We'll just live like we *were* born in a barn. Next time you come over, don't be surprised if you see farm animals."

Tenderly-ish, she answered with sage advice, "Suck it up, buttercup! Boys are noise with dirt on 'em. This isn't the worst of it. Just wait 'til they're teenagers. Those gross beasts reek!"

She was right.

Barn-Raised Boys

Eventually, I got used to the messes and noise. Looking back at my sons' younger years, I can now laugh about the chaos. It's fun to see people's reactions when I tell them about the time I did allow farm animals to live in the house.

One of my boys decided his chicks needed to stay in his bedroom because they didn't have enough feathers and it was too cold outside. Clearly, I had gotten over the need for a perfectly clean house by then and let him keep "Stinky" and "Toupee" in his room. However, I drew the line and insisted they go outside when their heads could reach over the shoebox, and they could jump out.

The elementary age is about when a boy's tender heart for animals becomes apparent. There is nothing sweeter than a little boy caring for a pet. My son became attached to his rats, hamsters, iguanas, cats, dogs, chickens, ducks, hedgehog, horse . . . Yikes! Maybe we were born in a barn? I wanted to encourage his love of animals, but it cost me quite a bit of money and pride to do so.

I wanted to encourage his love of animals, but it cost me quite a bit of money and pride to do so.

Did you know rats are bred for the express purpose of growing tumors? I learned the hard way they grow tumors ON PURPOSE. It's in their DNA. Just when your third grader falls in love with the "best rat ever," it develops a tumor, and you find yourself paying a veterinarian—who is laughing all the way to the bank—to perform breast surgery on it. Breast surgery. ON. A. RAT!

I don't feel that dumb, though. My sister-in-law fell victim to her son's pleading puppy dog eyes too. But her veterinarian was holistic, and instead of surgery, he prescribed aroma therapy. Again, for a rat. And she did it! Twice a day, she bathed the rat in the aroma of jasmine and a proprietary blend of clove, lemon, cinnamon bark, eucalyptus, and rosemary. It was the best-smelling dead rat ever.

Regular Mom Types

Some of my best friendships, many of whom I still have today, were made when my boys were in elementary school. Finally, a mother is no longer tied to the house with newborns and diapers and gets to be involved in fun activities such as the PTA, being a room mom, and finding out just how inadequate she is in comparison to the other moms that have it all together—or seem to. Prepare yourself, you are going to encounter many types of mothers at your child's elementary school. I've dubbed some of them "Earth, Wind, and Fire."

Mother Earth has everything under control. She is well-dressed with hair perfectly pulled back into a high pony—not a strand out of place. Her children are dressed in the latest styles. She creates clubs and sets up bake sales to raise money for numerous causes. She volunteers in the front office and in all four of her children's classes. Pinterest has nothing on her. She can plan a class party that would rival Martha Stewart.

On a field trip, she is prepared for any emergency. She'll have enough Band-Aids for the entire class, just in case. She makes nutritious home-cooked meals, and her family sits around the dinner table together every night and does devotions. Her children have never had sugar or preservatives. They participate in many activities, such as sports, music and art classes, 4-H clubs, theater, and chess tournaments—all at the same time. She will get everything on the Google family calendar done perfectly, but always complains about being tired.

Mother Wind has a tender heart for all things: people, animals, and plants. She loves everything and everyone with abandon. She will greet you with a hug and a compliment and hurts deeply if you don't see yourself the way she sees you: absolutely beautiful. Making sure you love yourself is her main focus today. Her children only eat organic. No juice boxes for them! It's only protein shakes with chia seeds and spinach for her tribe. She'll even bring enough to share with everyone.

Her children will be allowed to dress themselves to encourage their creativity. You never know what they might turn up wearing. It could be a school uniform or a cowboy costume. It doesn't matter to her. She's just happy to not be too late this time. She wants to help in any way she can, but first she must find her toddler who has wandered off—again. She is free-flowing and fun. All the children want to be around her because she will play with them for as long as they want and not tire.

Mother Fire lives the purpose-driven life. She has a way of doing things that is either the wrong way or the way you are going to do them—her way. She can be counted on to volunteer for everything. Her motto is, "If you want something done right, get out of the way and let me do it." With her in charge, everything is not only going to get done but get done well, even if it kills her. She will make sure every child is noticed and treated fairly. She will NOT let you down. Her children are well-mannered. They will shake your hand and address you politely as ma'am.

She can work a full-time job and still find time to make the most amazing cookies for the bake sale that Mother Earth has just voluntold her. She will be sure her cookies will make the most money for the cause. Why do something if you're not going to be the best at it?

Happy Hot Mess

And then, there was me. The Hot Mess Mom. While the other mothers were vying to outdo the other—perfectly dressed, everything done well, and all of God's children were seen, hugged, and loved—I rolled up to the school with a messy bun plopped on the side of my head, wearing doggy slippers, and wishing I had remembered to put on a bra. My children happily bounded out of the car, ready to take on the world.

I rolled up to the school with a messy bun plopped on the side of my head, wearing doggy slippers.

Well, except for the first grader—the baby. I had to force him to get out of the car. He'd given me fits all morning about anything and everything: what he was going to wear, whether he was going to put on shoes (I didn't even care at that point if they matched), if he was going to put on a jacket, zip the jacket, get in the car, and put on his seatbelt—EVERYTHING was a fight.

When we finally arrived at the drop-off line, his face (and mine) was red from screaming that he wasn't going to school, and I couldn't make him. The other kids rolled their eyes and jumped out, just happy to be free from the crazy. But not this one. Nooo. I had to get out of the car and walk around to open his door. As the other mothers gawked at me, I pried his vice-like grip off the door frame. Forcefully, I yanked him away from the car and carried him to his teacher who happened to be directing traffic and witnessing this episode of my crazy life.

Setting him down, ever-so-gently so she wouldn't call CPS on me, I spat out, "He's yours now!" and nonchalantly walked back to the car as fast as my doggy slippers could take me.

I can laugh at that . . . now.

Although hard and chaotic, I miss those days. We only get one shot at being a boy mom. Enjoy every stinky, silly, boisterous minute of it. God has entrusted you with an important task of raising the next generation of godly men. What an honor! The world needs you, mom. You've got this. Just tuck and roll with it. You're going to be fine, even if you can't take a nap anymore because your son will inevitably wake you up announcing, "I have something in my pocket, and it's alive. Guess what it is."

Oh, by the way, if you happen to be running behind one night, do NOT finish your son's first-grade math homework for him because he's going to get three wrong. Just a heads-up.

STACY SANCHEZ and her husband, John, have been married for over thirty-five years. She is a mother of three grown boys and one girl and grandmother of nine. Stacy is a pastor, author, and speaker. Her passions include all things baseball (Go Yankees!), the beach, and Bible study. Look for her new young adult devotional book *Diamond Dust: Lessons from the Ball Field* to come soon. Learn more about Stacy at **stacy.sanchez.com**.

This Rough Patch, Then Strawberries Come June

Abigail Wallace

DEAR BOYS,

Last week was a rough one, wasn't it?

We are *all* glad it's over.

It really was hard: four whole nights without dessert and five full days without a screen. I know it was hard for you. Being disciplined is hard for me too.

But if I have told you once, I have told you twenty times.

Discipline Means Love

Maybe I told you more times than was helpful and good. I got on a roll, and you heard me quote this verse so often that by the end of the week, you were quoting it too: "For the LORD disciplines those he loves, and he punishes each one he accepts as his child" (Hebrews 12:6).

I know it's hard to trust me. It's hard to believe that discipline is a sign of my love. I know that you miss Fortnite and ice cream. I understand. Honestly, I feel it too.

Because *no* discipline seems pleasant. I know that writing "I'm sorry" notes and forfeiting screen time did *not* feel good.

Skipping desserts does *not* feel like love. You have to admit that it was poetic justice, Son #1, when you had to pass on the National Chocolate Chip Day treats at the orthodontist's office because you had dumped your scrambled eggs in a rage. And the reason I made those very scrambled eggs was because it was a good food to eat with your brand-new braces.

Discipline left a bad taste your mouth.

Like Strawberries in May

It is almost strawberry season in Grandpa and Grandma's garden. Remember when you were little how we would go to their house, and while I would sit on the front porch and visit with Grandma you two would wander out to the garden? It wasn't so many years ago.

"Mama, look what I found!" you would yell, and proudly hold out a pinkish-whitish strawberry, the kind with just a tiny splotch of sunburn. Grandma warned you, partly for your sake, I think, and partly because she did not want a single one of her precious berries to be wasted. But you just could not wait. You both had to pluck a few before you knew.

I smile now as I write, remembering what came after your unauthorized picks.

Your pucker is what. You scrunched up your little faces and then—*Bleck!*—you both spat those unripe berries out.

But thank God that is not the end of strawberry season, and his promise is true. But you must let yourself be trained by this tough stuff, and not blow it off or give up. "And have you forgotten the encouraging words God spoke to you as his children? He said, 'My child, don't make light of the Lord's discipline, and don't give up when he corrects you'" (Hebrews 12:5). If you don't blow it off or give up during in this rough patch, I promise it will produce good fruit. I am one hundred percent sure this is true.

That is why Dad and I discipline you. That is why I tell you that over and over (Can we say it too much?): "Trust us. We love you. We're training you. It will be good." In big things and little things and all things in between, discipline means love. It means we are treating you as our dearly loved sons. For, "Who ever heard of a child who is never disciplined by its father?" (Hebrews 12:7).

Discipline means love. In the willful defiance that dumped those scrambled eggs upside down on the table like a baby might do. And in the screen time you stole late at night. And in the blurting-out, not-so-silly "joke box" talk by which you tormented your poor substitute teacher last week. Those things are why we are in this rough patch, together.

Like Scrambled Eggs, Sock Balls, and Toilet Seats

But we remind you of that truth in the small stuff too. Like when you have to place your mud-caked shoes on the mat and keep your napkin spread on your lap and look grown-ups in the eye when they greet you.

Down to the little things like lowering the toilet seat, screwing the cap on the Crest, and tossing your dirty socks—not sock balls—in the basket. Trust me, guys, these will make a future wife very, very happy.

Here's a little secret: when I tell you about how discipline means love, I'm talking to myself as much as I'm talking to you. Because this last week, these last months, and, honestly, the better part of this year have been hard for us all. Dad and I have had some painful, loving discipline too.

> Being trained by discipline—yours and mine—takes every bit of strength I've got and then some.

My friends say you guys have a strong mom. But I want you to know, sons, that being trained by discipline—yours and mine—takes every bit of strength I've got and then some. But we are in this together, you two with God and Dad and me. That means it will be okay.

Which explains why I saw more than the scrambled egg and catsup mess I scraped off the table when you left for school Monday. It's why I didn't cry about the "better off in an orphanage" comment you made as you walked out. And Son #2, I *did* see that teeny smirk when you said it. It's why the two lucky Tuesday afternoon phone calls—one from *both* of your teachers—when one of you yanked a classmate's necklace and it broke, and the other would not stop telling jokes in class even after the warnings. The teachers care. They don't want to see you go bad. And neither does God. That's why I didn't cry when those two calls came on the same day.

Thank God, I saw more than catsup and eggs and didn't lose heart. I also saw that in love, God was disciplining *me*. That is the only way I could shake off our utterly scrambled week.

Make no mistake. I am *not* writing this to make you feel guilty. I'm writing this note to remind you of what you already know: that Dad and I love you so much, and that's *why* we discipline you. In your heart of hearts, you already know that only sons *without* loving moms and dads could dump their eggs and taunt their teachers and get away scot-free. You've heard me say that I don't correct strangers' sons when I hear them belch in front of me, and I don't discipline rude kids I hear yell in the park, but I *will* definitely correct you.

Because I care immensely more about you.

Like Lion's Paw Love

Guys, do you remember the chapter we just read in *The Horse and His Boy*?[5] The part when Aravis and Shasta and their talking horses were racing hard to escape evil Prince Rabadash and save the Narnians? The part where their lungs were about to explode because they were pressing so hard? And where the lion suddenly tore at Aravis's shoulders?

I bet you do. Because when I read it at bedtime the other night, you both gasped.

But do you also remember *why* the lion wounded Aravis? It was to push her home. It was to keep her from a hateful enemy capturing or destroying her. It was to push her on to do the right thing, even when it was hard.

---

5. C. S. Lewis, *The Horse and His Boy* (The Chronicles of Narnia) (New York, NY: HarperTrophy, 1994).

Sometimes scares and tears and roars are needful for us too. Discipline drives us on in the right directions. It pushes us away from the dangers that would damage our souls and helps us get safely home. But in the moment, it is not pleasant. Discipline is painful. It hurts.

I feel it too. I could say disciplining you hurts me more than it hurts you. But I know you'd roll your eyes, so I won't.

Rarely do the really valuable things come easy.

Let's just say it isn't easy being your mom. I love it, but it isn't easy. Rarely do the really valuable things come easy. Since God loves me and wants me to look, act, and think more like his beloved Son, he gave me *you* two. Raising you guys helps grow me up into the Christlike lady I need to be—scrambled eggs, teacher calls, orphan talk, and all. That is all part of *my* story too.

Like Strawberries in June

God loves you guys more than you know. He wants you to grow into godly men with strong faith, great love, and soft hearts. He knew you would need a mom and dad like the ones you have. That is part of *your* stories, your painful and sweet stories.

God disciplines his children. We all felt that last week. But this is a brand-new week. We will move on. Because this is absolutely true: "No discipline is enjoyable while it is happening—it's painful! But afterward there will be a peaceful harvest of right living for those who are trained in this way" (Hebrews 12:11).

Remember those unripe strawberries from Grandpa and Grandma's garden that you promptly spit out? In a few weeks, come the middle of June, those sour pinkish-whitish berries will become heaven's sunshine transformed into the sweetest fruit. That is how it is supposed to be.

Dad and I love you, and so we must discipline you. God loves us, so he disciplines us. That is all how it is supposed to be. It tastes tart now, like strawberries in May.

But it will sweeten soon like strawberries in June.

I love U4VR my sons,

Mom

ABIGAIL WALLACE is a Scripture-soaked speaker, writer, and encourager. Her greatest joys come in helping others strengthen their hands in God. Abigail lives with her husband and two teenage sons in rural Wisconsin, where she enjoys fast walks, deep talks, chasing sunsets, and challenging the soul's status quo. Find her new book *Meek Not Weak* at Amazon and more soul- strengthening resources for strong moms at **abigailwallace.com**.

I'm Raising a Boy and Have Oodles of Questions!

Melissa Meyer

STANDING ON THE CORNER OF our street, I listened to a couple of robins having a conversation in a nearby tree. A slight breeze blew through my hair as I rolled my neck from side to side to loosen it up a bit. I had just wrapped up my workday, which involves sitting at my desk in my home office, tippity-tapping on my laptop until it's time to walk down to the bus stop to meet my kids.

"What should I make for dinner?" I wondered. Again. For the one billionth time. I would need to start preparing *something* when we got back into the house.

I knew what Bennett, my six-year-old, would eat for dinner. A corn dog. It was what he wanted for every dinner. He would eat a corn dog every day if I allowed it. But since I'm a *good* mom, he rarely gets more than four in a week. Don't judge—I firmly hold the line when he asks for a corn dog for breakfast. He won't give up on that one, despite a 0–1,095 record when asking. Why is he so persistent?

Finally, I saw the school bus making its way down the block, and soon my kids tumbled out in a burst of energy. They are literally the last ones off the bus every day, as we live three doors down from the last stop on the route. That's when I noticed it. *Another* hole in the knee of Bennett's pants. It wasn't there when he climbed onto the bus that morning. This was the last pair with no holes in the knees.

So, now, every pair he owned was officially a "play" pair of pants. Nothing nice left in the dresser drawer. I guessed he'd go to church in raggedy clothes after that. *When is spring going to arrive so he can switch to shorts?* I thought. *And when is he going to stop putting holes in every pair of pants? Do all little boys create holes in every pair of pants they own? Why do boys dive on their knees like that? How do I make it stop?*

No one told me that being a boy mom would involve so many questions.

How Do You Raise a Boy?

I grew up in a family of three girls. And I'm the oldest. So, yes. I'm bossy, responsible, and a big-time people-pleaser.

Growing up, I didn't really know what it was like to live with a boy. A male, sure. I lived with my dad. But I never lived with any *boys*. Smelly, loud, messy boys. Boys who think any poopy talk is hilarious and belch just to entertain themselves.

In my parents' home, there were dolls, twirling batons, and jump ropes that transitioned to boy band posters on walls, lip gloss, and *lots* of hairspray. Hey, my parents were raising girls in the '80s and early '90s.

> How do you let them live in their boy-like ways, nurture them, and allow their tough side to balance out their tender side?

My husband and I didn't find out the sex of our baby when I was pregnant. We wanted to be surprised and savored the anticipation. So, when I delivered Bennett, and the doctor declared, "It's a boy!" I knew I had a learning curve ahead of me. How do you mother a little boy when you've never lived with one? How do you let them live in their boy-like ways, nurture them, and allow their tough side to balance out their tender side? And how in the world do you potty train a boy? Clueless, party of one here!

My son is now wrapping up his kindergarten school year. Through lots of prayer for wisdom, patience, and understanding, I've come a long way in what I know about little boys. And one thing's for sure. God chose *me* to steward the life of my son. And even though I might have a lot of questions, I know the One who has the answers to the important stuff that really matters.

Why Is Everything Sticky?

There isn't a lollipop my son hasn't met that he didn't like. Or a balloon, for that matter. But it's the lollipops that make my world sticky. And the freeze pops. And the Tootsie Rolls. And the applesauce.

The back of the kitchen chair, the wall in the entryway, and pieces of a board game all have hints of sugary residue. And don't even get me started on the remote control. They all have a trail of stickiness as though Bennett is a slug, moving his way through the house with a sucker in hand. I just follow those sticky spots like breadcrumbs, and they lead me to him somewhere in the house.

Not only is my world stickier since becoming a boy mom, but it's a lot messier too. At a very young age, Bennett perfected the old "dump and run" move with any container of toys. Various piles of toy cars, tiny plastic animals, or LEGO blocks lie around my floors like colorful landmines. Sometimes, he wouldn't even play with whatever he dumped out. Apparently, it bothered him when something was contained and not spread out all over the house. I imagined his thought process went something like, *Order? What's that? Not on my watch! Order must be destroyed!*

It's like my mother-in-law always says, "Kids love chaos."

When he was a toddler and preschooler, I would ask him to pick up his piles. My battle cry quickly became, "You make the mess; you clean up the mess."

He would usually respond with pitiful wails of, "I'm too tired!" Now it's met with protests of, "But I was still playing with those!" Never mind that the piles of toys sat untouched for hours.

Sometimes, I wonder, *Will he ever learn to clean up his messes? Why do I need to ask him five times to do one thing?* That leads me to wonder, *Do I ignore God's voice as much as my son ignores my instructions?*

Who Will This Boy Become?

"Mom, watch this." Bennett lined up several toy characters from various kids' meals purchased from different fast-food restaurants. He knocked them toward him, one by one, into the bath water.

"Impressive," I wanted to say sarcastically. Instead, I looked down at the book on my lap and asked, "Do you want me to read another chapter?"

"Twenty-seven more chapters!" he declared. He always requests a ridiculously high number of something, be it chapters read to him or the number of chicken nuggets he wants served to him.

"Buddy, there are only three chapters left." And with that, I continued to read to find out what Junie B. Jones was going to do next in the story. This is our weekly bath-time ritual. He plays and sloshes around in the tub while I read a chapter book out loud to him.

Even though my son has been asserting his independence since he was old enough to say, "I do it," he often likes me nearby. If he's having a bad day, being nurtured by his mama is a healing balm to the sad or upsetting circumstances he may find himself in.

Always our big snuggler, Bennett gets his inner cup filled up by being close. He is my tenderhearted little boy who loves to give me hugs and high-fives several times a day. He would rather sit *on* me than next to me. Fitting on my lap is becoming a challenge because of the quick rate of his growth.

I know that Bennett's childhood years will scurry by, and all too quickly, I'll shockingly be looking up at my boy, who can grow facial hair and speak in a deep voice. It's hard to picture that specific vision right now when he's just a little red-headed kindergartner who bears a slight resemblance to Opie Taylor from *The Andy Griffith Show*.

So, until that day when the t-ball glove has been long outgrown and he no longer sleeps on a bunk bed, I will tuck the little boy moments into my memory. The only way to make time slow down is to appreciate this current phase of boyhood, resisting the temptation to look ahead to the next. And I'm sure I'll still have oodles of questions I'll ask myself and God, never being a boy mom with all the answers. None of us will ever have all the answers.

The only way to make time slow down is to appreciate this current phase of boyhood, resisting the temptation to look ahead to the next.

I'm fairly certain I'll shake my head at the memory of being irritated about holes in his pants. Because in the grand scheme of faith and eternity, stuff like that doesn't matter. And I'll ask myself, "How have I been so blessed to receive the privilege to raise such a wonderful son?"

MELISSA MEYER is a freelance writer for small businesses and entrepreneurs. Her business name, Bets & Ben Creative, is named after her children, Betsy and Bennett. She and her husband, Chip, live in Hudson, WI, with their children and two naughty kitties, Buddy and Oliver. When she's not writing for clients, you might find her avoiding housework by reading a novel, listening to a podcast, or enjoying "afternoon coffee" like a good Scandinavian should. **betsandbencreative.com**

10 Things I Love About Being a Boy Mom

Michelle Rayburn

I HAD MY BOYS ON THE same day, in different years, and I like to say I got my twins two years apart. I never once wished either of them had been a girl. Not that we've had a perfect life by any means, but I'm so grateful to be their mom.

I started a list of all the things I love about being a mom to only boys, and in minutes I had a dozen things and counting. The pros *far* outnumber the cons. I've narrowed that down to ten things related to convenience, creativity, and connection.

Convenience

Being a boy mom provides some convenience related to time and budget that I believe is unique to our situation, but a little disclaimer: I've never raised a girl. So, I have no idea.

1. Getting ready is faster. I consider myself pretty low maintenance when it comes to getting ready to get out the door, but nothing compares to how fast either of my boys could get ready for school. They could go from snoozing to cruising in ten minutes or under, depending on whether they brushed teeth. They'd throw on a t-shirt and yesterday's jeans, clean socks (maybe), the shoes they didn't untie last night, and they were off.

When they were small, I kept my boys' hair buzzed. It stayed cleaner, and we never had to brush it. It also helped in hunting for ticks after playing outside. Eeew. I'm starting to feel itchy all over now.

2. I have time to myself sometimes. As an introvert who loves a little time alone to read a book and sip an iced coffee, this benefit refuels me. When we went camping, Phil would often take the boys off for a hike while I had a little time to lounge by the fire.

When they got older, Phil started taking them on canoe trips, leaving me with a whole house to myself for a few days. Sometimes the quiet was just for an afternoon, where they went exploring in the woods somewhere or started a project outside. Other times, it involved my traveling to a conference over a weekend. I cherished whatever time I had. Even if it involved returning home on a chilly day to discover two grass-covered, muddy boys in the front yard with a makeshift slip-and-slide from a tarp and a garden hose. Dad was in the garage tinkering on stuff while he had them occupied.

3. I don't have to share clothes. Never in my time of raising boys has either one raided my closet or borrowed my favorite sweater. There was the exception for that whole week or two in elementary school where their feet were around the same size as mine before the next growth spurt, and someone used my shoes to run outside and squished down the backs.

On the other hand, I can't even count the number of times we rummaged through Dad's closet for a dress shirt, pants, suit jacket, or shoes.

4. They are cheaper to clothe. The clothes don't necessarily cost less. It's just that they wear the same five things over and over—or go stretches of days in one outfit. I know the amount of laundry that comes through would contradict this, but that's because they recycle clean clothes from the pile to the floor to the dirty laundry again. Much of what goes through a boy's laundry has never been worn.

If you've ever packed a boy for camp, you also know that all your neatly stacked coordinating outfits labeled by day will come home untouched. There will be one very dirty pair of socks, if you get them back at all, and one disgusting t-shirt and pair of shorts that foul up the whole works so much that you have to wash everything—unworn clothing and all.

Much of what goes through a boy's laundry has never been worn.

You'll have discussions about why it isn't a good idea to put on dirty underwear after a bath or why the jeans are now beyond hope and we must burn them.

Creativity

I love how two boys can be both alike and vastly different at the same time. Mine were not stereotypically rough and tumble. They didn't practice the sport of parkour in the living room, a game that reminds me of The Floor is Lava. They didn't bounce off the walls. Nor was either one hyperactive or exceptionally loud. But everything about their existence demonstrated creativity.

5. They're so imaginative. For my sons, playing Pay Day wasn't enough as a regular old board game. They decided to use items from their toybox as life-sized pawns to represent houses, property, careers, and all the actions and items included in a round of the game. Every G.I. Joe, car, boat, and stuffed bear or monkey got involved in growing net worth.

Similarly, when they got tired of the Monopoly game, they made their own versions. My favorite was Rayburnopoly, one where everyone in the extended family had representation. There was also a version for the Bible camp where Dad worked.

With the emergence of digital technology came creative filming of G.I. Joe wars and lip sync music and dance videos—some of which ended up on YouTube. Those have since been deleted because both are now high school teachers, and there are some things you hope your students never stumble upon.

6. We bonded over music. Music was a big part of my childhood, but I had no idea if my sons would be musically inclined or not. After all, my husband always says the instrument he played in school was the radio. From the time they could talk, they loved to sing with me—even in front of a crowd. Both took up trombone in middle school. My theory: boys are particularly drawn to instruments that can be manipulated to sound like a rhinoceros breaking wind. I liked it because it is a budget-friendly instrument.

My theory: boys are particularly drawn to instruments that can be manipulated to sound like a rhinoceros breaking wind.

From toddlers with toy drums to kids' worship CDs and sing-alongs, guitars, piano, and horns tooting in after-school practice, music has filled our home in both lovely and not-so-lovely forms. But it's all music to my ears.

7. They make me laugh. Before having boys—before meeting my husband, actually—I tended to be a bit straitlaced and serious. Being the only girl in an all-guy household has brought out a side of me I didn't know existed. They've inspired me to let loose and embrace lighthearted sarcasm, love puns, and appreciate well-timed antics.

They discovered already as preschoolers that if they could make Mom laugh, it neutralized a lot of fallout. On one of those early hikes Phil took with the boys (see number two above), he let them have suckers—because anything with Dad usually involved candy. I stayed at the campsite, reading, and when they returned, they greeted me, stickiness evident.

"I found a weaf," Dallas said. He raised his palm. A leaf stuck to it as if he'd learned a new magic trick to keep it there.

Not to be outdone, Austin fastened a leaf to his chin like a little green goatee.

Connection

Some of my most treasured and heartwarming memories come from the family connections—past, present, and future—with our boys.

8. Being like Dad. I enjoyed watching my sons try to walk in Dad's big cowboy boots or wear his cap. They dressed in matching denim jackets. Wanted to ride in the truck with him, have a toy motorcycle like his, and have their own tools or fishing poles and tackle boxes. But my favorite ways they became like Phil were not ones that were intentional.

Sometimes their mannerism or gesture would remind me of their dad, which made me fall in love with Phil all over again. They picked up on his laugh and the way he crosses his legs. How he stands with his hand on his hip. They also absorbed his patience and kindness, a servant's heart. I still see Dad in how they now treat their wives.

9. Built-in best buds. Although Dallas and Austin have different personalities and interests, they were best friends. I know that not *all* brothers experience this. Perhaps it's because we lived in the wilderness, far from the main road or the mailbox. Far from the kinds of neighborhoods where kids get on their bikes and ride to the park or to a friend's house. Yes, they had their own friends too. But at home, they were each other's best friend. And I didn't have to break up a lot of fights.

10. I get to raise someone's future husband. As a boy mom, I often fantasized about the day when I'd have daughters-in-law to balance things out. (Now that the day has come, I can say it was just as great as I fantasized.) I reminded myself when they were in elementary school and middle school that I got to have them for a little while, but their hearts would belong to someone else someday. I also took my responsibility seriously, raising future husbands, not just sons.

The bathroom they shared often looked like a truck stop restroom. And more than once, I found out after a guest (usually the mother of one of my piano students) had left that there was NO paper to be found in that bathroom. If someone reading this has been a victim, this is my public apology. We did our best.

I taught the boys to clean, especially the bathroom. There is still a checklist inside the medicine cabinet door with a little cheat sheet for which cleaning product to use and where. I also taught them to do laundry from around age eleven or twelve. Each had his own laundry basket in his room. When it was full, he could run a load. This significantly cut down on that laundry recycling issue we were having.

We also practiced dating skills by going on one-on-one evenings out with me. They couldn't drive, but they could plan where to go, open the door for me, engage in conversation over a meal, and pay the bill with a twenty I slipped them to take up to the register.

WHAT WOULD YOU ADD TO your favorites list? I haven't mentioned hugs and snuggles, smiles that melt my heart into a puddle, and other cute stuff. Because my boys are adults now. And they've read about all the mushy stuff they can handle here. But from one boy mom to another, we'll know that sons have a way of stealing our hearts forever.

MICHELLE RAYBURN is an author and podcast host who helps others find hope in the trashy stuff of life. She has an MA in ministry leadership and writes Christian living books, humor, and Bible studies. Together with her husband, they've raised two sons and gained two daughters-in-law—plus three granddaughters (go estrogen team!) and a grandson. Dark chocolate, an iced coffee, and a good book in the hammock top Michelle's favorites list. **michellerayburn.com**

Video Games, Bad Dudes, and Mom Anxiety

Abigail Wallace

"OH NO," I MOANED. "HONEY, PLEASE come. You need to see it now. It's really bad."

He came. I scrolled. And late Saturday night, we strode into our twelve-year-old's otherworld, where my husband, Jim, saw what I had seen:

Scotchlover16

RealDirtyDon

"No. Not good," Jim agreed.

We winced at the way-too-gleeful, Joker-like profile picture of a sinister, thirty-something male that happened to be one of Sam's gaming "friends."

Our eyes raced down the message thread until they landed on this:

"You there, Sam?" Scotchlover16 had written when—thank God—Sam was already in bed.

"'Sup Sam?" is all RealDirtyDon had said.*

Anxiety Hits

Last month, our school offered "Online Safety: What Parents Should Know." I didn't go. But I have heard the stories and read the tales of how unsuspecting adolescents get trapped. Then you see their faces on milk cartons and their names on the news. A coworker's niece had run off with an online friend, and it was over a year before she was restored to her family. By then, the damage was done. Yes, I do know about phishing and trolling. I know that perverts and creeps sneak into kids' sites seeking prey, not play.

Enter Scotchlover16 and RealDirtyDon.

Still, here we were, two middle-aged gaming novices. Truth be told, we were clueless. I'd never played this game before. We scoured the site in vain for more red flags, more signs of Scotchlover16 and RealDirtyDon enticing our son.

Just because we couldn't see the signs didn't mean they weren't there. These types are savvy. They don't leave tracks beyond creepy names and a few lines of chat.

As I tracked back into his playing history, I noticed something ominous: whenever Sam was on, Scotchlover16 or RealDirtyDon—or both—were on too. Just waiting for our son. Stalking. Prowling. Waiting.

That's when it hit. Anxiety got the best of me. Worry tied me in knots. I had every right to be concerned. Because bad things do happen.

My memory is not so short. I remembered that morning five years ago.

Flashback Sparks Worry

I'd just finished washing pancake syrup off the table. The boys had gone off to wash their hands. Now the one came back.

"Something bad happened, Mom. You don't want to know."

So ended our easy Saturday morning.

"I *do* want to know," I assured, kneeling before our second grader.

Then my seven-year-old showed me two of the most obscene gestures I had ever seen. I mean, in all my years, I had seen not motions so vile.

The sun went dark.

But only for about a minute, for I am an eternal optimist, ever a prisoner of hope.

"Maybe they're only innocent motions to him," I thought, "like when he was three, and he would use his middle finger to point at pictures as we'd read."

Interrupting my glowing internal narrative my darling added, "This one means a boy is . . . and the other one is what a girl does . . ."

Test positive. This dear son was infected.

The boy who watched G was exposed to X, or at least "Mature." This son with the sensitive eyes, the one too scared to watch plenty of cartoons for sheer "weirdness," the boy who would cover his ears to block the TV voice of a talking clay rabbit—this son saw *that*. He heard *that*.

My heart crashed into my gut.

In the hush, I whispered, "Buddy, where did you learn that?"

With his wide blue eyes to mine, his soft, serious voice to me, he answered, "It was Evan, Mom, on the bus. I don't think I should be his friend anymore. A big boy showed Evan, and he told me what it meant. But I don't know his name. He doesn't go to my school."

That's how my baby's tender mind was tainted. It is how innocence is lost. We can't go back and unsee. We can't rewind and unhear. What's done is done.

Which is why I knew that I had every reason to worry about these two bad dudes—this Scotchlover16 and that RealDirtyDon.

An "A Thrower" Activates

The Word of God is living and active, and at just the right time, at 10:55 p.m., a Bible verse came to mind: "Give all your worries and cares to God, for he cares about you" (1 Peter 5:7).

That verse reminded me of a message I heard the week before about the same verse. In fact, that's probably why the verse came to mind. The pastor first mentioned a new term for garbage men. He called them "G throwers," as in *garbage* throwers.

Then he asked, "Are you an A thrower?"

A what? I wondered too. "A" stands for anxiety, as in worries and cares and the sick feeling I had in the pit of my stomach after discovering Scotchlover16 and RealDirtyDon tonight, these two bad dudes, just waiting for my twelve-year-old to fall into their wiles. Right there, ready to expose him to more toxic words. Ready to pounce and carry him away.

"A" stands for anxiety, as in worries and cares and the sick feeling I had in the pit of my stomach.

I needed to throw some "A." *How* we throw our A is to pray. As in, "Don't worry about anything; instead, pray about everything" (Philippians 4:6). In other words, toss your anxiety. Pray.

In bed that night, we did. Together, Jim and I prayed. We gave our cares to God. My husband and I prayed about Sam's video game exposure and the wicked people waiting, and we asked for protection and safety. By grace, we obeyed.

As soon as we said our "Amen," we formed our game plan. We would take no drastic measures. Not yet. In the morning, we would talk to Sam—soberly and calmly. We could go from there. But first, we A throwers slept.

We slept so well that we overslept. Which meant we didn't have time for the talk.

Mom Wants Answers—Now

Our race to church left no time for anxiety. Not until I'd slid into the back row did the next wave of worry hit. Because anxieties and worries come back just like boomerangs. They came hurling back as I sat in the back beside Sam.

But since I *am* training to be an A thrower, and since on-the-job training is best, I did some A throwing. I prayed.

"Lord, please protect Sam. Please give us wisdom. I know you care. Amen."

Then, in the middle of "Joy to the World," right at "No more let sins and sorrows grow," I leaned over to Sam. I just couldn't wait.

"Sam, we need to talk about your gaming friends. You know, Scotchlover and RealDirtyDon? Dad and I don't think you should be their friends, even in video games."

Sam's eyes got wide. I hurried on.

"Son, did you know Scotch is a hard liquor? It is a very dangerous beverage. And, Sam, RealDirtyDon—you know that name just does not sound good. It sounds, well, dirty. Maybe it even sounds evil. I think these are bad dudes. I am very concerned, Son."

As the church sang on, I turned again to face Sam.

Anxiety Fades to Amusement

"Um, Mom?" Now Sam leaned over to me. He loud-whispered back. "Mom, Scotch is Nick's dog's name. Remember Nick, my friend from school?"

I did. But I wasn't sold.

"What about that profile picture? That isn't Nick."

"No, Mom, he just picked that picture because he thought it was funny."

Funny? Then again, what's funny to a thirty-eight-year-old mother might not match what's funny to a twelve-year-old boy. Granted.

"But what about RealDirtyDon?"

"Oh, Mom," Sam started to giggle. "Don is Donovan. He's sitting right there." He pointed up three rows and to the left. "That is him with his mom and dad. Mr. and Mrs. Brauckhoff are your friends. Dirty just sounded good. Kind of funny."

That's when the anxiety dam burst. Every ounce of "A" flowed out in the form of uncontrollable, wet-eyed laughter. We laughed and laughed and laughed—loud enough that the folks around us raised their eyebrows and looked back at us. And we laughed right on.

By the time it simmered low enough to sing, the choir was on verse four: "He rules the world with truth and grace, and makes the nations prove, the glories of his righteousness, and wonders of his love."

And wonders of his love. Indeed.

God's Care Reassures

We know this is not the end of the road. There will be more that is frightening ahead. There will be more worries to give to God. We A throwers, like G throwers, have job security. This side of heaven, mothers of sons will always have plenty of cares to cast on the Lord. Because there really *are* creeps and predators and evil men. There are older boys who know ugly, corrupting things on the bus. There *are* bad dudes.

> This side of heaven, mothers of sons will always have plenty of cares to cast on the Lord.

But there is also a God who rules this world he so loves with truth and grace, a God who wants to take our worries and burdens. "Give your burdens to the Lord, and he will take care of you" (Psalm 55:22). There is a God who cares.

Exhibit A? The mom in the back row that Sunday in Advent. The one whose relieved laughter spilled joyful tears in wonder of God's love. In wonder of a Father who actually calls his anxious children, including the ones with children of their own, to throw their every care upon him.

*Some names changed.

ABIGAIL WALLACE is a Scripture-soaked speaker, writer, and encourager. Her greatest joys come in helping others strengthen their hands in God. Abigail lives with her husband and two teenage sons in rural Wisconsin, where she enjoys fast walks, deep talks, chasing sunsets, and challenging the soul's status quo. Find her new book *Meek Not Weak* at Amazon and more soul- strengthening resources for strong moms at **abigailwallace.com**.

Raising, Rivaling, and Resolving

Kolleen Lucariello

IF I COULD PRESS THAT classic VCR rewind button and redo a few of my mom moments, you can bet that I would put up with the awful squeaky sound for a few do-overs. As a mom of two boys with completely different personalities, I wasn't always quick to exhibit the patience I admit I now have with my grandchildren.

I now realize that in my less-than-finer moments, I failed to take a breath and enjoy my boys as individuals. Each brought so much to the table—literally; one would bring the conversation listing the highlights of the day, while the other would bring the comedy. The older was structured and hoping to gain approval; the younger comedic and hoping to gain attention.

When Boys Are Being Boys

The motto "Boys will be boys" became lost on me when I witnessed the sentiment often used to shrug off misbehavior. However, I was never more aware of the underlying truth of this perspective than on those days when I could not anticipate the antics of my boys.

Such as the day I walked into the house to discover our black cocker spaniel with a fresh coat of butter. From the top of her head to the tip of her tail, she'd been completely smothered in the greasy fat. Why, might one ask? Because *boys will be boys.*

There was also the day I walked out the back door to discover the trampoline we once owned had been moved to the end of the house, and the ladder now stood on the deck, resting nicely against the roof. All in preparation for the fun the boys, along with their friends, would have while thrusting one another from the peak of the roof onto it. "Can you imagine how high we'd bounce, Mom?"

Did you know boys can easily use their garbage cans for toilets in the middle of the night when they're too tired to walk all the way to the bathroom? If you discover you have a damp carpet and an ant problem but can't figure out why—you're welcome.

Sometimes there are simply no words. Well, when you can't find them, there is always, "Umm, no."

I can't bring myself to talk about the shenanigans we interrupted through the years while lifeguarding at our backyard pool. Some things are better left unsaid. Sometimes there are simply no words. Well, when you can't find them, there is always, "Umm, no." No explanation needed because *boys will be boys.*

When Moms Monitor Conflict—and Their Hearts

As parents of these two remarkable sons, their father and I had a responsibility to monitor our response when the boys were being mischievous. While, at the same time, allowing them to mature and develop their personalities without encroaching upon the individuality their Creator had designed for them to be and become. This can be easier said than done when personalities create conflict.

Because our boys had such different personalities, we found it necessary to adjust our approach to each one on an individual basis. For example, when one complied with the instruction to not touch their sister, the other would hold his finger inches from her face and declare, with daring eyes, "I'm not touching her."

There always seemed to be a sequence to these moments. One would heed the warning, while the other would ignore it, and then when the consequence ensued, we'd listen to their list of *our* failings as parents. Of course, unfairness and favoritism were usually mentioned on the list.

This, however, was one area we were committed to never allowing to creep in and become a truth between us and our boys. Thankfully, this was highlighted after I read the story of Isaac and Rebekah. As I read from my Western perspective, I felt semi-confident that favoritism contributed to the outcome of the relationship between their two boys, Esau and Jacob.

Their story is found in Genesis chapter 25. After pleading with the Lord for his wife to conceive, we learn that when she did, the pregnancy was more than she'd bargained for when "the two children struggled with each other in her womb" (Genesis 25:22). The boys were in conflict even within the womb, and it was too much for Rebekah to understand. When she asked the Lord why this was happening to her, God's answer was not, "Because boys will be boys."[6]

His answer was, "The sons in your womb will become two nations. From the very beginning, the two nations will be rivals. One nation will be stronger than the other; and your older son will serve your younger son" (Genesis 25:23).

When You Realize You're Raising Rivals

Isaac and Rebekah had been gifted with rivals to raise. Of course, we aren't told of the early years when it was possible the boys were just being boys. It doesn't seem farfetched to imagine that—as rivals—the struggle went straight from the womb into the home and never left. After all, Jacob was born grasping at his brother's heel.[7]

6. Genesis 25:21–22

7. Genesis 25:26

As I see it now, it seems quite possible God told Rebekah of the rivalry to better prepare her for raising two boys that were going to struggle. Perhaps God wanted these parents to understand each son had a different call and purpose. Therefore, they would need to guard themselves against the pull of favoring one over the other based on personality.

I wonder if they had remained focused on what God had planned for each son if they could have been spared some of the family drama and heartache favoritism spawned.

That's not what happened, however, because each parent favored one son over the other. Dad had his favorite. Mom had hers. Isaac loved Esau *because he* was the wild one—the outdoorsy type—while Rebekah loved Jacob *because he* was the quiet one—the content-to-stay-home type.[8] Ouch. Every time I read this story, I wonder if they had remained focused on what God had planned for each son if they could have been spared some of the family drama and heartache favoritism spawned.

When Siblings Resolve Rivalry

I am grateful that Isaac's love of Esau and Rebekah's love of Jacob wasn't left out of their story, as it helped shape ours. This insight encouraged us to become intentional in squashing any inclination of favoritism when we factored in the "because" of our boys. It was *because* Isaac appreciated what Esau brought to the table (quite literally) that he loved him. It was *because* Rebekah appreciated what Jacob brought that she loved him.[9]

8. Genesis 25:27–28
9. Genesis 25:27–28

From my perspective, as a mom of two boys with different personalities, I have a sense this added to the rivalry between the boys rather than resolved any of it. And from beginning to end, I wonder why would anyone want to add any more to this rivalry than was already there?

God had given Isaac and Rebekah a blueprint for each son that I see as an opportunity to help prepare these boys for the future. There would be a struggle. They would be rivals. But was it necessary for the parents to align with one son over the other? This was the lesson I wanted to learn as a mom of two boys. I never wanted to be accused of loving one son over the other *because of* the personality God had given to each one.

When God Builds Your House

Not too long ago, I pulled out one of my prayer journals from years ago. As I skimmed through the yellowed pages, my eyes fell on my handwritten reminder that "A house is built by wisdom and becomes strong through good sense" (Proverbs 24:3). I reread my prayer that asked God for the wisdom necessary to teach our children all God had to say about them. He clearly had far better things to say about who they were than what I ever could.

Perhaps we could avoid the downfall that came upon Isaac and Rebekah through appreciation for our boys' individuality. My prayer was that each son would be content with their birth order and that I'd avoid raising boys who spent years apart because of resentment. This would be one of my do-overs; I would rewind to the moments I spoke to them out of *im*patience rather than revealing *his* patience.

I would rewind to the moments I spoke to them out of *im*patience rather than revealing *his* patience.

Good sense recognizes that God knows them from the inside out and loves everything about them. Unfortunately, if we become like

Isaac and Rebekah, we may only know them from the outside and love them *because* of what they do rather than who they are. (If you are wondering what that sound is, I just pressed the rewind button). Unfortunately, there were moments when I lacked the good sense to look past the do and focus on the who.

Good sense guards against the wish that one was more like the other. It is true that boys will be boys, and there will be squabbles and struggles as personalities clash. And yes, there will always be some rivalry between them as they learn to step into the qualities God gave to each one. They can discover God's personal plan created just for them if we, as parents, protect our own hearts from favoring one over the other.

When Parents Avoid Unnecessary Rivalry

Of course, like Isaac and Rebekah, we may relate and connect with one more than the other, but they *loved* one over the other. Loving our boys as individuals might protect our family from the devastation of pitting one against the other. And though our children may want to imply there is favoritism when confronted by the consequence of choice, we can rest knowing each will receive fairness if we have set a guard over our hearts.

> I'd have more patience, and I'd seek to enjoy the differences in our personalities rather than irritation at our differences.

I may not have always displayed good sense when the boys were being boys or learning how to wrestle out conflict. I may have even used the sentiment "Boys will be boys" a time or two as an excuse to overlook some misbehavior. I'd have more patience, and I'd seek to enjoy the differences in our personalities rather than irritation at our differences. However, I would never change them. They each brought laughter (and a few tears) as well as individuality within our family.

Boy moms may never fully understand why boys do what boys do, but they can raise them to think about what they are capable of *because of* their unique handcrafted design by their Creator. My boys may have come from my womb, but they came from God's heart. Every mom has a tremendous influence on her sons. She can teach them principles of how to overcome conflict and what healthy rivalries look like and encourage them to go and build the future God intends for them.

In those moments when words for their shenanigans fail, take a deep breath. And as you exhale, give thanks to God for allowing you to be a boy mom—and that no one was hurt.

KOLLEEN LUCARIELLO is wife to Pat, mom to her three married children, and Mimi to six of the finest grands. She's co-executive director of Acti8Her, Inc., a ministry that is connecting women in relationship, building confidence in leadership, and developing courageous faith. She is the author of *#beYOU: Change Your Identity One Letter at a Time* and is a contributing author to *Life, Repurposed* and the WordGirls Collective *Sage, Salt & Sunshine*. Follow her at **speakkolleen.com**.

Moving, Moods, Mudbugs, and Maturing

Gina Stinson

HE CONVINCED HIS SEVENTY-YEAR-OLD GRANDMOTHER to ride the four-wheeler. Gently, he helped situate her on the ATV and then hopped on in front of her to drive. Jo—our nickname for her—placed her arms around him, holding on with all her might. I'd like to think his twelve-year-old common sense prompted consideration as he rode the twenty-six-acre property with her, but I was afraid, from the look of Jo when she returned, that he had bumped her up and down one too many times. She was frazzled and looked more like Maxine on the front of a Hallmark card than our Jo.

But you never would have known it by his wide grin. He announced proudly, "We're back!"

And there, Jo carefully removed herself from the four-wheeler and said, "Well, we can mark that off the bucket list!" We all chuckled, but later I would slip Jo two ibuprofen to help with the inevitable discomfort headed her way.

Shortly thereafter, life would take a turn. Our family would move nearly five hours away, Jo's health would decline, and a heaviness of a tropical storm would ravage our new community. My son, who once was carefree and hilariously happy, would experience some difficult times, and his faith in God and others would be tested.

Moving

After we'd lived in the same town for almost ten years, my husband accepted a new pastoral position in Southeast Texas. We underestimated how difficult this would be for our children. Moving tweens and teens away from their friends and all they have known since childhood brought tears, frustration, and depression. To date, it has been the most heartbreaking experience for me to watch my kids navigate.

Tucker, more social than his sister, began the transition with a more positive attitude. He was determined to make new friends, enjoy the outdoor living and hobbies that the coast would bring; he would try new foods, and overall embrace the experience. Those last few days as we packed the house up, cleaned our property, and loaded our moving truck were also sprinkled with sharing meals, reminiscing, and lots of hugs with old friends. Overall, he handled things without the tears and anguish his sister felt.

Until the final day.

His heart was broken for what he was losing—friends, familiarity, family close by. The reality of the move pierced his heart.

We rolled down our gravel circle driveway one last time, crammed packed in our vehicle. Music playing on the radio. We paused as we pulled out—sort of exhaling all the tiredness and achiness in our bones. And that's when I heard the sniffles and then the sobbing. Understandably, he was grieving. His heart was broken for what he was losing—friends, familiarity, family close by. The reality of the move pierced his heart.

Moods

As we settled in after the move, I noticed highs and lows in Tucker's moods and attitude. Making new friends happened quickly, and our new church family welcomed us and immediately loved my children—making sure they felt accepted, praying for them, and showing genuine concern for a smooth transition to their new home, town, and church.

I felt as though all I ever did was correct, correct, correct, with an occasional "Wait until your dad gets home" and "You're grounded" added in.

But with all the trying and helping, Tucker was still a typical twelve-year-old middle school boy who was moody and pushing the envelope with things like talking back, cleaning his room, interacting with his sister, and being generally argumentative. I felt as though all I ever did was correct, correct, correct, with an occasional "Wait until your dad gets home" and "You're grounded" added in.

I bought books to read, both for him and me. I didn't like this phase and wanted to do whatever it would take to get out of it as quick as possible. But there was no end in sight.

Tropical Storm Imelda ripped through our town, dumping forty-four inches of rain in less than twenty-four hours. Our house was severely damaged, causing us to take residence in our church for four months. Living together in a small classroom is not the ideal situation for any family of four. While terribly grateful, Tucker lost his privacy, his room, his routine—more losses after an already hard year.

The next year would bring the loss of his grandmother. After a battle with dementia, our Jo passed away. She and Tucker had a special bond and had enjoyed years of storytelling, candy consuming, dollar store shopping, and sleepovers. While Tucker understood she was whole and healed now, like all of us, he grieved the loss of her beautiful life. Another loss. Another heartache.

Soon, we were smack dab in the middle of COVID-19. Life shut down all around us. He was watching his dad perform weekly funerals and minister to the sick in ways that were different and difficult. The seriousness of the days we were living in was heavy, and Tucker was feeling it.

Mudbugs

I remember when I noticed that maybe things were starting to take a turn for the better. On a particular Sunday, we had been invited over to a friend's home for a crawfish boil. My family had yet to fully embrace the fine delicacy that "mudbugs" are, and so, although we accepted the invitation, everyone was pretty reluctant.

Once there, the kids went through the buffet line and loaded up on various foods. Much to my surprise, both had a pile of crawfish to try. After a quick lesson in peeling, deveining, and other crawfish information, my kids began devouring their crustaceans.

We sat on the back porch that day, and finally, I saw some hope, a dash of normalcy, a tiny indication that they were starting to adapt to their new home. One small step.

Maturing

Life had been unpredictable, harsh, and consuming. That is the solid truth. But in between all the hard times, were also some very good times. New friends were made. God showed off in supplying for us in tangible ways. Old friends came to visit. Tucker learned to play the guitar. We took a family vacation. Our home was fully repaired. And eventually, we were able to have conversations about the goodness of God with Tucker.

Honestly, I mothered a lot of years in the lane of protecting my kids from the bad things that happen in life. While there will be things that I don't talk to my kids about because they don't always need to know, talking to them about hard times is no longer one of those topics. Some of the best conversations I have had with Tucker are based on decision-making, planning, trusting God, believing God will work things out for Tucker's good and God's glory—and these conversations didn't start because our lives were perfect. Instead, many were sparked because of hard times, grief, and frustrations.

> Honestly, I mothered a lot of years in the lane of protecting my kids from the bad things that happen in life.

Mental health issues like depression and anxiety are rampant in the lives of preteens, teens, and young adults today. The last few years have placed an enormous amount of pressure on them to navigate in waters that even we, as parents, have had to learn as we go. I couldn't ignore these hazards.

Even years later, as his mom, I want Tucker to be as healthy as he can be. I want to help him learn how to place boundaries around himself so that he can experience the freedom to make good choices, have good mental health, and react with a Christ-like spirit—based on reality, not fear or depression.

Rehearsing our victories has become one of my favorite things to do with him. When negative or disappointing circumstances come our way—while still operating in the truth of the hardness of those times—I enjoy talking about God's faithfulness and goodness to us in the past. Because it is okay to be both happy and sad at the same time. It's okay to mourn and dance. It's okay to laugh and cry. There is a time for everything.

The sniffles in the back seat of the car as we pulled out of our driveway for the last time were signs we lived a life worth missing there. Grief for a grandmother gone indicates she was loved and cherished. The sadness of loss in any way brings opportunity for reflection, truth, and yes, even eventual celebration.

Taking the time to be honest in these hard days keeps us grounded in reality. In this life, there will be trouble and hard times. But also, looking for brighter days ahead reminds us that God is the source for hope, healing, and joy. Although we still have our difficult days, the truth of brighter days brings perspective to the grief of the past. In these truths, Tucker is learning to cope with good and bad situations with more clarity.

So, the move, the moods, and the mudbugs remind me that one way to protect and prepare Tucker for the future is to look for the truth in the pain and the blessings in each situation. These middle school lessons are great for moms too.

After years of living in fear and defeat, **GINA STINSON** is reclaiming every day for God's glory. She's a pastor's wife of thirty years and mom of two young adults. Gina is a storyteller writer who enjoys retelling wonderful ways God is at work. She's incredibly easy to locate on social media or at **ginastinson.com**. Otherwise, you'll find her at the hobby shop wandering the yarn aisle looking for inspiration for her next project.

It's the #Boymom Life for Me!

Stacy Sanchez

HAVE YOU EVER BEEN HIT in the face with the aroma of something that smelled like three-day-old fish left out in the sun, a forgotten egg from last Easter, and bathroom tile from the city subway? Congratulations! You must be a middle school boy mom. Get used to it. The intensity of the smell heightens the closer he gets to manhood. But be warned, so will the atomic mushroom cloud of body spray Prince Charming will use to cover the stench.

What happened to those pudgy little toddlers who followed me around like uncoordinated puppy dogs—even to the bathroom—and clung to me as if I was their personal jungle gym? I miss the tender boy cuddles and sloppy kisses. They sure loved their mama! They still love me, just not until after the video game is over. And, trust me, DO NOT interrupt a video game right before they're about to level up. This mistake will wreck the mood in the whole house for the rest of the day.

Oh, how they've grown! What once were precious newborns waking up two or three times a night to be fed, comforted, or just be near me have morphed into awkward pre-teens who sleep in as late as possible, unable to be roused from their slumber even if a bomb goes off.

(Unfortunately, their bedrooms look like a bomb did go off!) Those tiny fingernails I clipped and curly mops of hair I brushed out of their eyes, they now beg to paint black and dye blue.

Are You Absolutely Sure?

I fondly remember a picture that once hung prominently in my home. The drawing portrayed three boys covered in mud, each causing one kind of trouble or another. One boy was at the top of a tree—his knee skinned. Another had a frog in his pocket. The third was sticking out his tongue. On it was written "There's a Special Place in Heaven for the Mother of Three Boys."

No truer words were ever written! I definitely earned that special place in heaven with my three, and I am expecting a girly drink with an umbrella in it when I get there! I raised three boys and one girl, all of whom are grown. Two of my sons now have three boys of their own. I have nine grandcherubs: eight boys and one girl. This family sure can make those XY chromosomes!

I didn't set out to be a boy mom. In fact, with my first pregnancy, the sonogram tech swiped over my stomach with the wand and announced, "It's a girl!"

I questioned how she could be positive.

"Oh, I can tell." She reassured me. "In fact, if it's not a girl, I'll owe you a trip to Hawaii."

"Ok," I countered. "You're the professional."

I believed her and prepared for the arrival of my daughter. You can imagine my shock when I heard the doctor proudly announce, "Congratulations! It's a boy!"

I'm still waiting for that trip to Hawaii.

My second and third pregnancies were different. There was no doubt I was having boys in those sonogram pics! When they arrived, there were no surprises. Thank God! I was a boy mom three times over and have never regretted one messy, noisy, boisterous minute of it. I was born to be a boy mom.

Do You Smell That?

Middle school aged boys are a special breed. I think aliens come down to earth on their twelfth birthday and steal their brains. My boys didn't get their brains back until around the age of twenty-five, maybe thirty? Until their brains return, you will be in for a rollercoaster ride of hilarity and frustration. Don't be surprised if, in the middle of disciplining your son, you need to turn your head (or crawl under a church pew) because whatever he did to land himself in trouble was funny.

Middle school aged boys are a special breed. I think aliens come down to earth on their twelfth birthday and steal their brains.

Trigger warning: you just may choke on your iced frappe when I recount this "if it wasn't so funny, you'd be toast" moment.

One Christmas Eve, we attended my mother's church in a retirement community. The sanctuary was decked out for the holiday. Poinsettias adorned the pulpit, greenery and ornate bows draped the windows, and an elegant chandelier spread shimmering rays of candlelight around the room. (Think Hallmark Christmas movie here. But no one fell in love.)

As the congregation held candles, the choir closed the service with a lovely rendition of "O Holy Night." Just when the soprano hit the crescendo of "Ohhhhh niiiiight deviiiine," my little bundle of twelve-year-old no brains—not so subtly—decided THIS was THE perfect moment to inquire, "Does anyone else smell tuna fish? I smell fish."

I couldn't have shushed him any quicker or crawled under the pew any faster. The looks on those proper ladies' faces told me they'd never had boys. Well, they missed out. Because it's fun.

Where Are All the Forks?

Being a middle school boy mom is not for the faint of heart. Bodily function jokes will be told ad nauseam. Various animals—dead or alive—will be found in pockets, hidden in closets, or appear in your washing machine because you forgot to check their pockets. Silverware will go missing. If you're lucky and happen to find a piece, it will have been used to dig a pet graveyard.

I found myself saying things I never thought I'd have to, like: "No, you may not make a bomb! You made a what? Where is it?" And "Stop pulling the heads off of your sister's Barbies and telling her zombies snuck into her room in the middle of the night and ate their brains." Or "Just because you're a boy doesn't mean you can pee anywhere. The church has a bathroom for that." And my favorite: "No! I won't smell that!"

Was I Just Voluntold?

Even though his changing interests are as fickle as a weathervane, I learned to love and became an expert in his activity *du jour*. If not already, mark my words, you will become involved. It's inevitable. Becoming a coach, team mom, scorekeeper, or chaperone is in your future. Every league or group is always in desperate need of volunteers, and you will soon become "voluntold."

> As the mother of a middle school boy, you will become an expert at treating acne and broken hearts.

You may not enjoy sitting at your son's games in the freezing rain or the blistering sun, cheering the team on to glory—secretly hoping they lose so you can go home and marathon *The Not-So-Real Housewives of Make Believe*—but you know in your heart these are the memories you will look back on and cherish. Even if yet another dinner was from the drive-thru while you screamed, "Hurry up and eat! We're late!

As the mother of a middle school boy, you will become an expert at treating acne and broken hearts. This is the age when your little bundle of joy becomes a big bundle of complicated hormones. Girls no longer have cooties right at the time boys become their most awkward. During middle school, his need for independence grows. To mature, he must push away from you, which is painful for you and confusing for him. One moment he wants to sit and cuddle, and the next he won't want to have anything to do with you, especially if he's around his peers.

A middle school boy is desperate to fit in and incredibly insecure about what is happening to his body. What he wears or who he hangs around will be his utmost concern. This is the phase of looking cool in front of his friends. This will mean he cannot be seen hanging around with you. Sorry, but you are no longer cool. Don't even bother trying or you will get the "Gah!" and eye roll.

Did He Steal My Heart?

No matter his personality, whether your son is outgoing and loves sports or is quieter and more sensitive, preferring to spend time in his room reading, he will need to pull away from you to mature into a man. Here's the unspoken secret: you know you're doing this boy mom thing right when he doesn't need you. Ouch!

> Our job is to raise these boys into men who don't need a mommy. (Your future daughters-in-law will love you for it.)

Sadly, our job is to raise these boys into men who don't need a mommy. (Your future daughters-in-law will love you for it.) This starts in middle school with pushing your boundaries. He'll hang out with friends you prefer he didn't and won't do his schoolwork so he doesn't look like a geek. Or, as my son did, push a boundary just to scare me by riding his boogie board out past the waves and farther than the surfers—just to prove he can. (Thankfully, there was an understanding lifeguard who heard my protests and watched him carefully.) You are their safe place to try, fail, fall, and get back up to try again.

The wonderful thing about being a boy mom is that though he must grow into a man who leaves you, he will always have a special connection to his momma. Yours was the first face he saw. Yours was his first kiss. You were the first woman he loved. No one can replace you.

So, throw your hair into a pony and wear that faded #boymom hat with pride! Never forget you are doing incredibly important work. Yours is a significant calling of raising boys the girl moms can trust. If anyone can raise a stinky boy into a great man, it's you, sister!

STACY SANCHEZ and her husband, John, have been married for over thirty-five years. She is a mother of three grown boys and one girl and grandmother of nine. Stacy is a pastor, author, and speaker. Her passions include all things baseball (Go Yankees!), the beach, and Bible study. Look for her new young adult devotional book *Diamond Dust: Lessons from the Ball Field* to come soon. Learn more about Stacy at **stacy.sanchez.com**.

Teens

Four by Camper and Three by Canoe

Michelle Rayburn

TWO ROADS DIVERGED IN A wood, and I took the road to electricity and memory foam. He chose the road less traveled by. And took the boys with him—eventually.

My husband has loved wilderness camping from the time he was young. To me, there was something backward about loading up a pile of gear, driving for six to eight hours, unloading, canoeing into the unknown, unloading and portaging everything for a mile or more, then reloading just to canoe into more of the unknown.

If you're as unfamiliar with portaging as I was, it means carrying the boat and paraphernalia over land to get to another lake. I wholeheartedly agree with one family member who once said of his canoeing and portaging experience, "I could just as easily disassemble a Buick, carry it across here, and reassemble it."

We compromised on the camping thing when my husband wanted our boys to experience the escape from real life for a weekend. I had not agreed to Boundary Waters adventures with the marriage vows, so he'd have to save that sort of camping for trips with friends, siblings, and cousins until our boys were old enough to accompany him. Some aspects of real life appealed to me. Like showers. Running water. Air conditioning. Bathrooms that have walls and flush levers. I liked my curling iron and my dishwasher too.

Not one person in our family of four voted for a weekend of shopping or crafting—ever. So camping it was—for multiple weekends every summer. We transported more stuff than we'd ever need up to a state park somewhere along a lake or river and set up our antique pop-up camper—the very one I'd camped in with my grandparents as a child.

Tenting with Tent Worms

On one of those trips, Phil had backed the camper into just the right spot, and we started setting up. I remarked on how beautiful the site was and how the boys were going to love the beach—my typical wife chatter to counterbalance how bossy I'd been about the backing-up part. That's when I noticed our companions.[10]

A fuzzy worm crawled across the picnic table. And another one. There was one on the bench, too, and then there was one on the camper.

A fuzzy worm crawled across the picnic table. And another one.

"What's up with these caterpillars? Where are they coming from?"

"I'm not sure," Phil responded, not really looking at what I was talking about.

"No. Seriously. They are everywhere!"

By now, the camper and the Jeep and the lawn chairs had caterpillars all over them. That's when I realized it was raining worms. Tent caterpillars plopped from the trees like big fuzzy green raindrops.

---

10. Story first appeared in: Michelle Rayburn, *The Repurposed and Upcycled Life: When God Turns Trash to Treasure* (New Auburn, Wisconsin: Faith Creativity Life Books, 2012) 77–79.

I got back in the Jeep.

"I'm not coming out."

"It's not that big of a deal," Phil's voice oozed with as much compassion as a bill collector.

Neither of our boys seemed bothered by this development. They'd continued their exploration of the campsite without a blink. It also apparently didn't bother them that the only restroom facilities in our loop were vault toilets. I'd be driving the Jeep over to the shower house rather than squatting over a pit, that was for sure.

I dug a magazine out of my backpack and waited while Phil set up the camper and covered it with the ugly blue tarp. Then he assembled the screen tent, which also happened to be blue. When Phil stood back with his hands on his hips to admire his handiwork—aka our redneck shelter—I saw my opportunity to make a request.

"Can we please run to the Walmart I saw a few miles back? I just need to buy a hat. I don't want these stupid worms in my hair." I figured it was the perfect double-duty stop since they sold hats *and* had flush toilets.

That weekend, I spent my cooking and relaxing time inside the screen tent, watching the shadows of caterpillars crawling on the outside of the canvas and running around with my wide-brimmed canvas hat whenever I needed to exit the shelter. I scrutinized caterpillar shadows inching across the tent tarp each morning after the sun rose—while I debated staying under the covers for the day. I finally convinced Phil to pack up before dark on our last full day and pull out a day early. No one complained, but I have a feeling they'd had enough of *my* complaining.

Making Memories

Until the boys were old enough for "real" camping, we made memories together at campgrounds all over the Great Lakes area—despite my discomfort. We squeezed inside our camper to play cards in rainstorms and hiked to the bathhouse for countless middle-of-the-night visits with a youngster. Despite crummy weather and lack of sleep, the net gain from a weekend was always a heap of fun. We changed flat tires along the highway and had the brakes on the Jeep go out while barreling down a hill into a town. Phil was able to buy enough brake fluid to get us the last few miles to the campground, and the next day, he got a ride into town to get parts so he could replace several brake lines right at the campsite.

We made memories in random parking lots on unplanned stops while Phil lay under the Jeep fixing something, and the kids and I stretched our legs or dug through the snack box and tried not to eat up all the s'mores chocolate. The boys eventually got old enough to help him.

We made memories in random parking lots on unplanned stops while Phil lay under the Jeep fixing something.

We now play old videos for our daughters-in-law of our character-building camping days. We chuckle at the interactions between our preschool-aged boys. In one video memory, Dallas is attempting to "burn" a marshmallow—his term for roasting one—but he keeps shaking his head and brushing at his face.

"Got bugs by you?" I ask.

"No. Smoke," Dallas says.

"Ohh. Smoke's in your eyes, honey."

Little brother Austin asks, "Is some in mine?"

"I think you'd know," I say.

Dallas solved that one later by wearing sunglasses, even after dark, to keep the smoke out of his eyes.

Building Bonds

Being a boy mom is about figuring out what works for us so that we can connect with our sons without losing our minds and also without skipping great opportunities in favor of pure comfort. If you're an adventuresome mom who sees tent worms as delightful campsite visitors, you'll have a different hurdle of your own to get over, I'm sure.

Boys are not as likely to sit across a table from Mom and have a heart-to-heart. But they *are* willing to pipe up from the back seat on a long road trip to somewhere. As they grew older, those conversations got deeper. The topics changed from discussing what type of wheels a passing truck had to favorite movies and books. We talked about their week at summer camp and learned the silly songs they'd picked up.

As they grew older, those conversations got deeper.

And then in middle school, the conversations shifted into more serious tones as they developed the maturity to handle weightier topics. For example, saying a heartbreaking goodbye to Grandma when the oncologist ran out of options for her cancer treatment. Then to a season of change that same year. "We're going to be moving for Dad's work." New friends, community, school, house, church. Chats morphed into things related to spiritual growth and discipleship as they took steps of faith.

And then the stage where they were, at last, old enough to go camping with Dad in places Mom would never go. Conversations around campfires with smoke in their now acne-dotted faces—chats saved for Dad alone. The birds and the bees. Stuff Mom wouldn't get. Stories about topics Mom wouldn't approve of. Things Mom would never say. While they rested on rocks and roots in a tent on the forest floor, I slumbered on memory foam and watched chick flicks to my heart's content.

The earlier adventures had taught us to pivot when life doesn't always go the way we'd planned. On one of our camping trips, Phil decided to sterilize the pudgie pie maker by shoving it down in the coals for a little while before we put the bread and cherry pie filling in. He busied himself with chopping more firewood while I prepped the ingredients at the picnic table.

When Phil eventually lifted the tool from the coals, molten metal dripped into the fire, and he had nothing but a long metal stick left.

There were a few tears of disappointment over learning there wouldn't be any of the hot, sugar-coated pies they had looked forward to. From a young age, we discover that disappointment is part of life, don't we? Bad stuff happens. But we also learn that it often makes us stronger and better people—families that stick together and problem-solve.

In the family tug-of-war over summer recreation, moms of only boys will likely do more compromising. The rope will probably move far in the sons' direction before you land on something you agree on, but you'll all win. I think of the opportunities and conversations I'd have missed if we hadn't all found something to love about camping.

And now I get to hear of their adventures when they come back from their guy trips. Like how they managed to cook for a week after forgetting key utensils at home. Or how they could feel the electricity from a lightning strike travel through the tree roots beneath them. No thanks! Or how they got a stranger to text me a message from a satellite phone to let me know they were alive when a windstorm made it impossible to canoe out on the day they were supposed to show up at home.

Some parts of camping are best left in a place called Ignorant Bliss. The rest are part of the boy-mom legacy of character-building, immune-building, family bonding.

MICHELLE RAYBURN is an author and podcast host who helps others find hope in the trashy stuff of life. She has an MA in ministry leadership and writes Christian living books, humor, and Bible studies. Together with her husband, they've raised two sons and gained two daughters-in-law—plus three granddaughters (go estrogen team!) and a grandson. Dark chocolate, an iced coffee, and a good book in the hammock top Michelle's favorites list. **michellerayburn.com**

Defusing Fear and Exploding Faith

Pam Fields

THREE O'CLOCK IN THE MORNING. "Do you hear crying?" I asked my husband.

No response.

"OK then, I guess it's my turn to see who woke up."

Half asleep, I walked down the hall and quietly waited outside each child's bedroom to see where the noise was coming from. It was the strangest thing; the noise wasn't coming from anywhere. The crying was gone, so I went back to bed. After lying down, again I heard crying. It was a steady whimpering.

Lighting the Fuse

There I went, down the hall once more to listen at the door of each room. I just couldn't figure out where it was coming from. Finally resigned that it was my imagination, I climbed into bed.

I have no idea what made me get up one last time or what drew me to the sliding glass door leading to the patio. It must have been the Holy Spirit whispering to my heart, "Don't give up. Keep looking."

As I peered out, I spotted the tearful display. Our eighteen-month-old son was curled up with Solomon, our old golden retriever, sobbing.

Relieved that I finally located the mystery cry, I went outside to rescue my son. His astronaut footie pajamas were damp from his adventure. When I pieced it together and retraced what must have been his steps, I figured it out. For some reason and in some way, Ben had opened the window, crawled out of his crib, and gotten outside. This was unbelievable, as he was only a toddler. Not only did he have to get out the window but scale down a few feet, then cross gravel and go around the house in the rain before ending up with the dog. I marveled at God's protection over my young son and for his design of "a mother's intuition." Baffled and incredibly thankful for my child's safety, I finally found rest.

These little ones kept us on our toes, and we had our hands full with five young children. Sometimes others offered us a break. One evening, our pastor and his teenage daughter volunteered to come over to babysit so that my husband and I could go out to dinner. When we returned, Pastor Greg, clearly amused, explained how Ben had challenged him.

Though he was only four years old, Ben stood his ground, fully convinced that he could physically overtake Pastor Greg when one of his instructions didn't match the normal routine of our home. The match-up was reminiscent of the ancient scene of David and Goliath, and Ben was undaunted. He was simply unafraid to call out any inconsistency or injustice that occurred under his watch.

Watching It Spark

There were a lot of things I wasn't prepared for as a mother, things that no one warned me about. One of those was the creative genius of children. In elementary school, Ben rigged a bungee cord to a tree and tied the other end to his belt loops to see if he could "bungee jump." Sure enough, it worked until every single belt loop was broken on all my children's pants. When multiple kids showed up and asked me to take them shopping to buy new "pants with belt loops," I started to ask questions. Then, I laughed.

Since I wouldn't replace their loopless pants, they adjusted their methodology. After scrounging around the garage, they jerry-rigged the bungee cord to a bicycle innertube to lie through at their bellies that would hold them while catapulting out of the tree. Ingenuity is the mother of invention.

There were a lot of things I wasn't prepared for as a mother, things that no one warned me about.

My boys regularly created swords, shields, and body armor from tin foil and cardboard. Instead of getting angry whenever the foil went missing from the kitchen, I bought another roll. Several rolls. Occasionally they would change focus, and instead of the weapons, they created "jet-packs" and astronaut suits out of empty two-liter bottles, duct tape, and other supplies that they recovered from around our home. Eventually, they ended up with boxes of their own creative supplies.

The best gifts my children ever received were supplies to fuel their imagination. Some days, they were able to be kept busy inside, gluing popsicle sticks together with hot glue guns or making models out of spaghetti and miniature marshmallows. I spent many hours reading to them while they worked with rapt attention on a LEGO project on the floor. By middle school, creative problem-solving was in full swing.

Though Nerf guns are fun, they can be outgrown. So, what's a young man to do with his Nerf collection when it has served its purpose, and he now has an interest in the next level of weaponry? Well, if you are my son Ben, you do some research and create "mods." Modifying Nerf guns to have the power of an Airsoft gun is a challenge, but that's just the beginning. With a little work, those Nerf guns can be engineered to shoot Airsoft pellets as well.

At times, I was frustrated when I looked at the financial investment that we had made in Nerf and Airsoft, only to see them splayed out on his desk with springs, gaskets, and plastic shavings everywhere. In retrospect, I had such a limited view of what was being created within my son. His skill in understanding and taking apart mechanical devices would someday be instrumental in what God had called him to do.

Nearing the Artillery

I had never heard of a "ghillie suit." Perhaps it's new to you too. After being well-informed of the structure and purpose, I was a mom on a mission for supplies. After a few weeks of combing thrift stores, I had gathered up enough materials to make it happen. I had no idea that a young man could have the interest and patience to sew leaves, sticks, and random woodland objects to a piece of netting to create a disguise.

The ghillie suit, camo clothing, and modified Airsoft guns were only a start, and they soon made way to the transformation in our backyard. The creations that he once made on a small scale were bound to level up. Though he is an adult now, the twelve-foot Airsoft towers built with free wooden pallets remain in the backyard, long overgrown with weeds. I'm certain there are still some pits out there as well, left from trap-making, and that hole that was in the process of being dug—all the way to China.

For hours at a time, Ben would lose himself in our pasture, setting up battlefields and armaments. Whenever he had the chance, he gathered his friends to practice maneuvers and hold mock combat. Sure, they played rough, and there were some minor injuries, but as they stood up to the challenges that they created for themselves, I saw young men grow in resilience, strength, and character.

As they stood up to the challenges that they created for themselves, I saw young men grow in resilience, strength, and character.

I will never forget the winter when we discovered mice in our pantry. Having a house out in the country has its ups and downs. The mice were part of the downs. It was all-out war to rid our home of the pests. As Ben worked on his homeschooling, he kept an Airsoft gun at his side. When he spotted a mouse out of the corner of his eye, math time was over, and it was on to target practice. Generally, he was able to dispose of the dreaded creatures quickly.

However, there was one day when the mouse was faster. I walked in on decorative pillows being hurled, couches being tipped, and all manner of chaos underway. Each time the mouse escaped and went into hiding, two brothers would toss the furniture to expose it. There was no way that the mouse would survive this fight! Sure enough, the boys won. They were my heroes!

There were many occasions that demanded the call of duty from my boys. Ben was undaunted by the dangerous and gross jobs. When the chimney needed cleaning, he was on the roof, working with his twin brother to prepare it for winter. If there was a stench of death creeping through the floorboards, Ben would suit up and crawl beneath the house to locate and retrieve whatever animal had lived its last moments below. Though it worried me, he would stop on the side of the road to help strangers with a flat tire or car trouble. Always looking for places and people who needed his help. His mind and his body were always prepared for action.

He would stop on the side of the road to help strangers with a flat tire or car trouble. Always looking for places and people who needed his help.

Detonation

It's no wonder that this son, before graduating from high school, drove himself to the recruiter's office and pledged his life for the defense of our country. While he was at boot camp, I became familiar with the training and challenges of a United States soldier. As much as the fear and concern for his safety alarmed me, I knew that this was what he was meant to do. He was a man of grit and honor. His life was a training ground for the work and service that the Lord had called him to.

At every point in his life, Ben had pushed the boundaries of risk and safety. Through every situation, God had protected him.

No work in the military is for wimps. Every job is essential, and every service member a hero. Just as I was getting used to the idea of infantry and its inherent risks, Ben reclassified and trained for a new job. He had joined the Explosive Ordnance Disposal (EOD) unit. When he left for his training as a bomb technician, I knew that all those years of ingenuity and fine-tuned skill had a purpose. The risky play and rugged challenges that he thrived on as a child and teen would have been the very things that anchored these brave choices for his future.

When I asked him why he wanted to defuse bombs, this was the way he explained it to me. "It's not a job for a married man. It's not a job for a dad. I'm single, and I can do it. Besides, here's the way I see it: if I do it right and defuse 'em, I'm a hero. If I get it wrong and die, I'm with Jesus. I can't lose."

Learning to trust God with my son didn't happen overnight.

Learning to trust God with my son didn't happen overnight. Through his childhood and youth, the Lord was preparing me. He was teaching me to recognize his hand of protection covering my boy. Though, as Ben's mom, I still have concern for his safety and diligently pray, I know that God's sovereignty is over his future.

PAM FIELDS is the wife of Andrew, mother of nine, and grandmother of four. She's always had a heart for encouraging moms in their walk with the Lord and in their mothering journey. She enjoys sharing testimonies on her podcast *The Mom Next Door: Stories of Faith*. When Pam has some free time, you can find her at coffee with friends or planning her next family gathering at their home in Cookeville, Tennessee. **TendingFields.net**

Where the Wild Things Were

Becky Melby

MY HOUSE. THAT'S WHERE THE wild things were. Yes, I'm referring to my four sons, but also to a menagerie of feral animals, both dead and alive, that found their way into our home. Or, in several cases, into my sons' stomachs. But I'll ease you into the wild things and start with the domesticated ones.

There are things no one ever warns boy moms about. Things like—guinea pigs and waterbeds don't do well together. You'd think the boy who named the furry little thing "Chainsaw" would have figured that out. Guess that's why those vinyl mattresses came with little vinyl patches.

Another thing they don't tell you is that having pets may force you to lie to your children. Like when your dearly loved pet husky kills the hamster that escaped its cage. The hamster that was dearly loved by a five-year-old. "I'm sorry, honey. I know you miss him. We'll keep looking." The day did come when we finally told the truth. Said boy was thirty-five at the time.

If anyone advises you to opt for a low-maintenance pet, read the fine print first. Hermit crabs sounded like the perfect choice. No need to walk or groom them. They stay put in a box or aquarium. No one warns you that the little buggers are nocturnal and will claw at the sides of their dwelling. *Scratch, scritch, scratch.* All. Night. Long.

> If anyone advises you to opt for a low-maintenance pet, read the fine print first.

Fish. Doesn't get much lower maintenance. A pinch of food every day. Once or twice a month, you nag a boy to clean the tank. But we got some tagalongs with the goldfish. A couple of tiny, harmless snails. Kind of cute as they climbed the glass sides of the aquarium. But the next week, there were four snails, then eight. Then one day, a boy said, "Look, Mom, they're hugging each other!" No one ever tells you that when some snails "hug," they can both get pregnant. Culling the snail herd is an endless job, and pea-sized escargot makes for a tedious meal.

Things with red eyes and naked tails should be in the "wild" category. Unfortunately, pet store owners disagree, and when the fifteen-year-old boy who wants one is taller and broader-shouldered than his mom, you might as well give in. So "Celia" went everywhere with our oldest son, riding on his shoulder or in his pocket. If visiting someone else's house (after clearing it with the host, of course), Scott would throw his jacket on the floor, and incredibly, Celia wouldn't wander off of it. I'll admit, I did kind of warm up to her. Naked tail and all.

Speaking of Naked Tails

The rat is a good segue into the wild things.

Every Christmas, our church held a progressive dinner. My husband and I offered to host the dessert portion, and a woman who was new to our congregation, a person I barely knew, volunteered to help. So the two of us left the main course early and drove to my house. It was dark. Our front door was lit only by the pale glow of the porch light. I reached for the door handle and gasped—in tandem with the almost stranger behind me. On a ledge next to the door and leaning against the siding was a flat, frozen opossum. Naked tail, beady red eyes. Dead as a doornail. My feeble response? "I have boys."

Nothing makes a parent prouder than a teen who wants to go on a mission trip. On the last day, our son Scott and his youth group were scheduled to return from Jamaica, and we eagerly awaited the arrival of the two vans bringing them from the airport. Finally, the first van arrived. The side door slid open, and a girl jumped out. Her first words? "Scott ate a live gecko!"

The story we were told was that Scott had picked up the small, wiggly lizard and dangled it upside down by its tail, asking if anyone dared him to swallow it. Of course, the kids cheered him on. (Later, there were rumors of Jamaican dollars changing hands, but we discounted these since no church-going teen would ever consider taking bets.) As the story goes, there was one mature voice of reason in the group. Their adult leader, a man we, for some reason, still consider a friend. His reaction? "Don't do it, Scott. Don't eat it. Don't. But if you're going to, let me get a video."

That video still exists. Unfortunately, the statute of limitations on allowing a minor to swallow live lizards has probably run out.

> When a mom is panicking over a child's safety, a call to the police might come out a little different than she intends.

Panic Makes a Mom Say Funny Things

The most infamous animal story in our family is the one about the terrifying animal that stole into our house one night and attacked our oldest son. When a mom is panicking over a child's safety, a call to the police might come out a little different than she intends. As in, there is a difference between saying "There's a wildcat in our house!" and "There's a wild cat in our house." If only I'd had a camera handy to capture the looks on the faces of the officers who arrived, clearly frightened, ready to defend us from a cougar.

It all started with the same teenaged son who owned a rat and ate a gecko. A pathetically thin barn cat had found its way from the farm across the highway and into our garage. Scott felt sorry for the poor thing and decided to give it some food. For supper that night, I'd made baked potatoes stuffed with cubed ham and cheese sauce. Scott took some of the leftovers and gave it to the cat—by hand. The feisty little thing tried to nip his fingertips but didn't draw blood. Not then, anyway.

It all started with the same teenaged son who owned a rat and ate a gecko.

Unbeknownst to us, there was a rip in the bottom corner of our screen door. Around ten that night, after all of us were in bed, we heard Scott yell. The cat had come in the house, up the stairs, and into his bedroom. He tried picking it up, but the skittish cat would have none of it. So Scott went downstairs, got some cheesy ham, and lured the cat to him until he could grab it.

He started to carry it down the steps, feeding it all the way, but the moment the ham ran out, the cat went nuts, flew out of his hands, and raked its claws down Scott's bare legs. That's when we heard the yell and sprang into action, Dad and son trying to corral the little monster in the bathroom, and Mom making a frantic call to the police.

Though the officers shot patronizing looks my way as they stepped into the bathroom and spotted their tiny prey, the screeching, flailing, and yelling resounding from behind the door they closed was proof they were not at all prepared for wrangling our three-pound "wildcat."

They finally captured it in a cardboard box. By law, since the cat had drawn blood, it had to be confined at the Humane Society for ten days for observation. At the end of that time, I got a phone call. "The cat can be released now. Would you like to keep it?"

Um . . . no.

Why Boys Need to Walk on the Wild Side—Sometimes

It's been eighteen years since our youngest son left home. But the stories still live on. And every once in a while, when our sons are all together, they'll let slip a tale they've kept from their parents for decades. Like the one we just heard about the camping trip where a copperhead was ready to strike at Jeff, our second son, but Scott, then in his early twenties, shot it just in time. And then skinned it, added some Cajun seasoning, and cooked it up for supper.

"Did Jeff eat it?" I asked.

"No. He couldn't even bring himself to taste it. And he slept in his car that night and couldn't even let his feet touch the ground."

Stories. Our boys need them.

It's hard to let them strike out on adventures. We long to protect them from the wild things. But if we protect them too much, they won't have stories to tell their sons. And their sons' sons.

When the men in our family gather, tales of wildcats, pet rats, and rattlesnakes get passed from generation to generation. As my grandsons grow toward manhood, they add their own stories to the wild and colorful tapestry they are woven into.

Take it from a mom of four boys who is now grandma to ten grandsons. Give your boys the gift of wild things.

Within reason, of course.

BECKY MELBY has been married to her high school sweetheart for fifty-one years. They are the proud, and still somewhat exhausted, parents of four amazing sons who have blessed them with four beautiful daughters-in-love and fifteen grandchildren. Becky has authored and co-authored twenty-six inspirational novels and novellas. For more information, find her at **beckymelby.com** or on Facebook.

Head Held High

Denise Loock

BALLCAP PULLED LOW OVER HIS forehead and shoulders hunched under the weight of his catcher's gear, Jeff trudged toward the car. My son's posture suggested his dream of playing on the high school baseball team had evaporated in the afternoon heat.

Disappointment stabbed my heart. For weeks, I had begged God, "Just let him make the team." My husband, Mace, had watched a few practices and intrasquad scrimmages. Behind home plate, Jeff handled pitches well—scooping balls from the dirt and throwing them accurately to infield players. His base-running instincts were good, but his stocky frame slowed his speed. At the plate, he was an average hitter. His stats included far more singles than extra-base hits.

Jeff had survived the first cut, but today the coach announced who made the roster. The other boy vying for the catcher's position was bigger, stronger, faster. He'd played travel ball for years. Mace and I doubted Jeff was a better player than that boy, but would the coach want a backup catcher on the squad? We hoped so. We prayed so.

Jeff opened the back passenger door and shoved his baseball bag across the seat. He slammed that door, then yanked the front passenger handle and slid into the car. His face was beet red—normal for my redheaded, fair-skinned boy when he'd been out in the sun. But the way he slouched in the seat and averted his eyes told me that anger—or was it shame?—stained his cheeks.

Head down, he said, "I got cut."

"I'm so sorry, Jeff."

The tears came. He swiped at them with his shirt sleeve.

A battalion of cliches about failure and perseverance paraded through my head. Not one of them could triage the gaping wounds in Jeff's ego. For months, he'd talked about making the freshman team. He had played community baseball since he was six years old. He'd attended the high school varsity coach's summer camp for years. He practiced hitting several times a week at the local sports club. At a high school of over 4,000 students, the probability of making a sports team was low, but that didn't discourage Jeff. He and his friends were confident they'd all make the team.

But he didn't.

He and his friends were confident they'd all make the team.
But he didn't.

Triage for a Wounded Ego

We drove home in silence. I didn't know what to say, and he didn't want to talk. As we pulled into the driveway, he said, "Mike got cut too."

I should have been sad for Mike, but I was glad for Jeff. At least he wouldn't have to live through this heartache alone.

As soon as I turned off the car engine, Jeff opened his door and walked into the house. I didn't call him back to get his gear. By the time I entered the kitchen, he was stomping up the stairs to his room.

Leave him alone, I told myself. Nothing you say to him right now will help. Nothing. I walked over to my mom's old rocker—my prayer spot. I closed my eyes, breathed deep, and whispered, "Lord, don't let him sink into depression or some other dark place. Protect my boy." Feeling calmer, I phoned Mace and told him the bad news. He agreed with my plan. All we could do was pray for God's guidance and wait for Jeff to talk it out.

A few minutes later, the phone rang. "Hello?"

"It's Rita. Mike's mom."

"Jeff's devastated," I said. "I'm sure Mike is too."

"He's out in the backyard whacking his baseball bat against a tree."

"Maybe that's what Jeff should be doing, but he's up in his room, music blaring." I chuckled, then released a long breath. "I don't know what to say to him."

"Not much to say right now, but Mike asked if Jeff could come over and spend the night. Might be good for them."

Of course. Jeff didn't need his mom. He needed a friend. "That's a great idea. I'll ask him and call you back."

Pain Management

"Have a good time," I said as Jeff got out of the car. Backpack slung over his shoulder, he walked toward the house, head lowered. Mike came out onto the porch to greet him.

My shoulders relaxed. The tension in my chest eased. I shot a prayer heavenward. "Lord, please help these boys navigate this pain."

On Saturday afternoon, Jeff called and asked if he could spend another night at Mike's. "He's got Super Mario Galaxy, and I've won three times. Plus, his dad said we could go to Angelo's tonight." Normally, Mace and I would have said no. Our family went to church on Sunday morning. But saying no to a hot new video game and his favorite pizza place? This time we said yes. Jeff sounded happy on the phone.

When I arrived to pick up Jeff on Sunday afternoon, Rita came out to the car. "They've been laughing all weekend. This was the best thing for them."

"Thanks so much for asking."

"Now if I can just get Mike to go to school tomorrow."

"I've been thinking the same thing about Jeff."

A Little TLC

Mace had not returned from his meeting when I went up to Jeff's room to say goodnight. "Tomorrow will be a tough day. But if you don't face your friends tomorrow, every day after that is going to be harder."

"I feel like such a loser."

"I get that. But what we feel isn't who we are. Not making the team hurts. It's gonna hurt for a while—maybe a long while." I made eye contact with him. "But you are not a loser. Trying out for the team was risky. You took that risk, which makes you a winner. So hold your head high tomorrow when you go to school."

His expression said, "You're my mom. You have to say that."

I fought the urge to quote a Bible verse. Instead, I laid my hand on his arm, closed my eyes, and prayed, "Lord, give Jeff the strength to go to school tomorrow. Amen."

I fought the urge to quote a Bible verse. Instead, I laid my hand on his arm, closed my eyes, and prayed.

When I opened my eyes, Jeff remained silent. Had the prayer helped or hurt?

I patted his arm again. "You're a good catcher. Hang on to all the praise your community league coaches have given you. Maybe Mr. Peterson will be your coach again this year, and Mike'll be on your team."

"He's not going to play community ball. He's done with baseball."

"That's a shame. He loves baseball. So do you. I hope you'll still play. I'm sure your dad does too."

"Can you make waffles for breakfast?"

Waffles were a Saturday treat, when the whole family ate breakfast together. But if waffles got him out of bed in the morning, the extra effort was worth it. "Absolutely. And I'll drive you to school so you don't have to ride the bus."

"Thanks, Mom."

Recovery Regimen

Jeff was up before I knocked on his bedroom door the next morning. Mace had already left for work, and the school day for our daughter, Kelsey, started an hour earlier than Jeff's. I didn't want to hover over him, so I wiped the counters, emptied the dishwasher, and refilled the cat's bowl while he wolfed down several waffles in silence. He wore his Derek Jeter jersey, and next to him lay his favorite Yankees ballcap. I hoped the ensemble made him feel like a winner.

I let Jeff tune in to his favorite radio station in the car. I didn't dare start a conversation—afraid that anything I said would shatter whatever confidence he had mustered to make it through the day. I prayed, though, begging God to give Jeff something to feel good about.

When we pulled up to the high school entrance, I said, "I'm proud of you, Son."

He didn't make eye contact, but he nodded before he opened the door. I watched him walk toward the entrance, backpack slung over his shoulder, Yankees cap pulled down low over his face. But he held his head high.

DENISE LOOCK is an author, speaker, and editor. Her stories have been published in Chicken Soup for the Soul and A Cup of Comfort compilations. She is the co-author of the Restore devotional collections and the founder of **DigDeeperDevotions.com**.

So-and-So's Mom

Joni Topper

ONCE YOU HAVE KIDS, YOU no longer need a name of your own. You become so-and-so's mom. My name used to be Joni. Then I became simply Rodney's mom. Most of the time, that's been fine with me. The honest truth is, there has seldom been a time in my son's life when I was not either so proud of him I could bust or so mad at him I could bust *him*.

Sometimes when people talked about him using terms of endearment, my husband and I would look at each other and shrug. We wondered who they were talking about because their words didn't match the kid we knew. He was a better form of himself for other people than he was at home. Raising him felt like riding a roller coaster without a seatbelt.

Homework Detail

We used the divide-and-conquer method to get him through high school. I spearheaded history. Ernest took on algebra. Rodney got so mad at me for telling him stories to make history come alive. "Don't tell me that stuff. I don't want to know it. I just want to memorize the answers."

In my opinion, if the questions replayed a story, the answers would be easy. He insisted that the extra information made it tedious rather than interesting for him. He preferred rote answers. I sheltered myself from the algebra tutoring as a form of self-defense. How Ernest got him through the numbers, I'll never know.

I sheltered myself from the algebra tutoring as a form of self-defense. How Ernest got him through the numbers, I'll never know.

Fortunately, Rodney loved athletics. I believe his coaches must have been designed in heaven because they offered him a great deal of grace. His coach instructed him on a Thursday that in order to play football on Friday, he needed to make at least an eighty-seven on his exam. Rodney was more than their quarterback. He was a self-assigned field coach. He knew where every player should be on every play. His coaches knew they'd miss his leadership should he be disqualified due to grades.

If the coach said he needed an eighty-seven, he would make an eighty-seven. Not one extra point, not one point less. I still do not know how he did it because his math skills were sketchy. My sister moaned that she had nothing to hold over her son's head. "You are so lucky that Rodney excels on the football and baseball fields if for no other reason than you can use it as leverage."

Friend Accommodation

As his teen years dawned, Rodney asked, "Can Carl* come spend the weekend with us?" I agreed and called Carl's mom. Little did I know, Carl's grandfather owned a professional sports team. They needed to send his bodyguard to check out where we lived before Carl could come.

After the bodyguard's inspection, Carl came for a visit. The boys played outside most of the weekend. We lived on twenty acres, and the area toward the back of our property included a fabulous rock formation that we called "the fort."

The week after Carl's visit, I overheard some women in the lobby at the post office where I worked. "Did you hear about the note the teacher confiscated? Apparently, Rodney and Carl were drinking last weekend."

The boys had filled a toy canteen with wine from the one and only wine bottle in our kitchen. They spent the afternoon drinking it back at the fort. This rude awakening to the reality of raising a high-adventure boy should have been a wake-up call for me as a mom. I seldom saw his antics coming and sometimes completely missed what I should have been watching.

I seldom saw his antics coming and sometimes completely missed what I should have been watching.

Rodney could never figure out how I discovered some of his indiscretions. Working in a small-town post office where you know most of the community, I did not have to be much of a sleuth. Information just leaked to me.

Our first child, a daughter, followed rules to the T. Her goal was to please, to excel, to cooperate. I grew up in a household with three girls. Rodney, my first lesson in the school of boys, seemed to know that I lacked both experience and savvy. I had no inkling what the boy might be doing.

When he started driving, Rodney seemed like a natural. I complimented him on his driving skills one of the first times I rode with him after he got his learner's permit. He looked at me and rolled his eyes. "Mom, I've been driving for years."

"How's that? You just got your permit."

"Mom, we don't let our friends drive drunk. I've driven lots of people home."

Bravado Tolerance

Rodney and his friend Jay* competed for the mirror in our living room. They wanted to stand in front of it and flex their muscles. Aside from causing the rest of the family to roll our eyes, their self-adoration felt like a byproduct of their hormones. They did not care if we rolled our eyes as long as we noticed their muscles. Confidence never waned in their teenage world. They just knew the universe was at their disposal.

When Rodney headed out for a destination that included girls, he splashed enough cologne on himself to fumigate the setting. "I called Jay and the guys and told them you've got the cologne covered for tonight," I would tell him on his way out the door. He thought I was kidding. If I believed they'd have listened, I *would* have called them. I wish cologne had been the only way they pushed the boundaries.

If solitary confinement had been a parental option, I might have exercised it for a few years. Holidays seemed to bring out the spunk in my over-adventurous son. I always felt a little relief when we settled back into mundane days after a special occasion. My daughter experienced a lot of stress, saying it was because she did not feel that I punished her brother enough.

If solitary confinement had been a parental option, I might have exercised it for a few years.

"Sometimes I have to just love the kid. I can't punish every breath he breathes." I knew there needed to be a balance between accepting who he was and correcting his blatant missteps while he blustered through those growing-up years.

ERNEST CAME HOME ONE DAY and found one of Rodney's friends inspecting the contents of our refrigerator while no one from our family was home. "You really don't have much here to eat." He reprimanded Ernest as though he were his personal staff. I took his cue and restocked the kitchen for the next siege of hungry boys.

Later, Jay's dad pulled Ernest aside in town, reaching for his wallet. "How much do I owe you?" he asked.

Puzzled, Ernest answered, "What do you mean? You don't owe me anything."

"I'm pretty sure I owe you child support."

"No. The boys ate at your house last month." Ernest shook his head. "We're even."

A strong bond formed between us and the parents of Rodney's friends. We traveled to all their ballgames together, ate before the games, and supported each other as fellow travelers on our parenting journey. Although my job required me to be at work six days a week at 6:00 a.m., I went to all those out-of-town games. The end of a ballgame became my favorite part. All those boys who raided my kitchen also left the field and headed straight for my arms for their post-game hug. Being their second mom filled my heart so full that I soldiered through the exhaustion of getting up early for work the next day.

One morning after a short night of sleep, my coworker asked about the ballgame the night before. "We won," I bragged.

"Who did you play?"

"I'm not sure. Their costumes were green, and the name of the town started with a C."

"Joni, they are not costumes. They are uniforms, and were you in Center Point or Comfort?"

"I don't know. I wasn't driving. I was visiting with the mother who rode with us, but I know we won." That was all the detail I could keep up with at the time, and it seemed adequate to me.

Opinion Battles

Parents' night during football season included walking out on the field with our son and being introduced as his parents. We escorted our daughter, a cheerleader, during the same event. When we dressed for the evening, Crystal complimented her dad. "You're wearing school colors tonight! You look great in that maroon leather jacket, Dad."

Just after she left the house to get ready for her cheer duties, Rodney came in to get his uniform.

"Dad, please tell me you are not wearing that jacket to the game. This is *not* a dress-up occasion. You can't wear that and embarrass me."

This scene is a perfect example of the difference in our children. They shared genes from the same parents and lived in the same home with the same rules. Both of them were in church every time the doors were open. Yet their style and goals and temperament followed no standardized form.

Ernest rocked the leather jacket to Crystal's delight and Rodney's objection. We had learned not to be blown over by our son's teenage thunder.

Mission Accomplished

Twenty-five years later, a room full of women hushed when I sympathized with another mom. "Oh, I feel your pain." My words came out instinctively. Pausing, I added, "I raised Rodney Topper." That mom's days overflowed with stress induced-trauma bought on by her brood of boys.

What I did not expect was to look up and see several women with their hands over their mouths. Someone voiced, "You are Rodney's mom? I love him. He helped us so much."

When the group dismissed, one of the ladies located me, asking if we could have lunch because Rodney meant so much to her family. She wanted to visit with his mom.

Rodney grew up. He became a successful Realtor whose name is synonymous with the Texas Hill Country. People love him because he listens to them. "You need your septic system pumped?" "You need a place to put some cows for a few days?" Whatever their problem, he directs people to the help they need.

Being a boy's mom equals being a blessed mom.

Being a boy's mom equals being a blessed mom.

Looking back, I recognize that those days on my knees praying were the most brilliant moments of my parenting. The psalmist said, "My help comes from the Lord, who made heaven and earth!" (Psalm 121:2).

I wondered, at times, if Rodney would even survive. God helped him to thrive. Today, my son loves me, and I love him right back. I still pray for him, but now I watch for his next great accomplishment.

* Name changed.

JONI TOPPER radiates God's glory by sharing everyday moments in riveting storyteller fashion—the inspiration for Joni's Morning Glory Ministry. Whether wearing her grandmother, author, or speaker hat, Joni's favorite description of herself is, "One who desires to look like Jesus." As a singer/songwriter, she emanates joy. Joni and her husband, Ernest, have been married for over forty-one years. Check out blogs at **Morninggloryministry.com**.

Midnight Snacks

Gina Stinson

When my children were young, I carried the weight and responsibility of diligent parenting very seriously. While I tried to be fun and enjoy the moment, I somewhat regrettably missed opportunities to just sit back and take in the everyday joys. There are only a few moments between diapers and driver's licenses, and I wanted to teach my kids every single thing I could in the brevity of those fleeting days. Little did I know, there's just no possible way to cram in a lifetime of learning in a mere eighteen years. But there is a way to enjoy both the years and the kids.

Sleep, the Underestimated Commodity

It had been a long day, filled with routine and a few added stresses. I was tired. After managing dinner, a few loads of laundry, math homework with Tucker, and wrangling our two large dogs, I was ready for a hot shower and a good night's sleep.

It was 10:15 p.m., and Bruce and I were headed to bed like two senior citizens making sure they got their eight hours of rest, knowing good and well, we wouldn't. Seems the older you get, the less likely "sleep in heavenly peace" is. And when you're parenting teens, it's even less likely. Sleep is the underestimated commodity every parent feels.

No one tells you about the sleeplessness that you experience as parents of teenagers. The waiting on them to get home, the time it takes helping to settle them down for the night, the tendency for them to want to have important conversations right as you're ready to climb in your king-size bed—then leaving you with random, ridiculous, and sometimes alarming thoughts floating through your head! These are the things they don't tell you in the baby books, but this, my friend, is the reality of parenting teens. Sleep is precious.

Midnight Hunger and Hilarity

Savannah and Tucker came into our bedroom for hugs and our routine goodnight chat. After they closed the door gently behind them, all I could think of was how wonderful it was going to be to get a good night's rest. I pulled the soft covers over me and snuggled under the heavy quilt, ready to sleep. Just as I was good and warm and relaxed, out of nowhere, Tucker, our fifteen-year-old son, bolted through the door again. With the excitement of Christmas morning, he asked, "Hey, Dad, wanna take me to Whataburger at 11:00 p.m.? We can go through the drive through and order breakfast!"

After the initial alarm of him barging in the room passed, and a few well-aimed pillows hit his head, we shouted a collective, "No!"

Laughter ensued. In Tucker's defense, Whataburger does have a delicious breakfast menu, but timing is everything, and these parents were tired. Tonight was not the night for a late-night breakfast.

If you've raised a boy, then you are keenly aware that satisfying their hunger would rank close to a biblical miracle.

Boys are bottomless pits. If you've raised a boy, then you are keenly aware that satisfying their hunger would rank close to a biblical miracle. So, this particular night, from the comfort of our bed, we offered a few solid solutions to his hunger hysteria: a sandwich, leftovers, even a frozen pizza.

He responded casually, "You know, if I have to make my own food, the kitchen might be noisy for a while. You really might want to take me to Whataburger for your own sanity." The tone in his voice was silly and mischievous. The look on his face—priceless. Bruce and I, in unison again, playfully shouted, "NO!"

Seconds later, we heard the pull of the cabinet drawers opening, and I quickly realized he was making good on his threat to make this a noisy experience. I waited with one eye open to see if this was going to be an extended performance or if he was just fooling around in the kitchen to be funny.

The clank of a large pot, the slide of the giant popcorn tin on the countertop, and the hollow saucepans being pushed together let me know loud and clear we were about to be treated to a drum concert! In a matter of minutes, he was playing beats and rhythms like a solo drumline.

Bruce and I stayed in bed. Trying to hold back the laughter. I didn't know whether to be impressed by his rhythmic ability and creativity or frustrated by the minutes he was knocking off the clock that I could be sleeping. For ten minutes, the drumming continued until finally, I intervened. Slowly I made my way out from under the warm blankets and into the kitchen where the concert was taking place.

As I peered around the corner, Tucker stood there with a large pot on his head, two pots strategically placed on the countertop, and the popcorn tin nestled carefully between his belly and the edge of the counter. There, with wooden spoons in hand, he was playing to his heart's content. It was a hysterical sight.

Laughter and Lightening Up

Perhaps because this year has been full of so many weird, unpredictable, and even sad moments, this incident was even funnier than it really was. But as I gazed at my near-grown son, I decided to be thankful for the humor, thankful he is talented, strong, and healthy. I gave thought to how different things could be.

How fortunate that this little noise was happening in my kitchen when others I know long for noise in theirs. I even considered that an 11:00 p.m. breakfast trip to Whataburger might be a good idea.

I'm learning that as my kids grow older, I have the choice to enjoy them or find them burdensome. Yes, there are times Tucker needs a firm hand to guide him, but there are also times when we can let a few things go and just be in the moment with him. His heart was playful and fun that night, not disrespectful or rude. When I take the time to carefully evaluate the motives and attitudes behind the behavior, I can respond in an equally responsible way.

I'm learning that as my kids grow older, I have the choice to enjoy them or find them burdensome.

Sometimes I make too much of a situation. I can take a moment that was meant as a light-hearted joke or tease and take it personally. I can over-analyze something until I've made a casual comment into a life-changing situation. This particular night, I could have easily taken his behavior and decided he was being disobedient, inconsiderate, and disrespectful when really, he was just being funny.

The night could have ended so differently. Instead of looking deeper, I could have blown up, exasperated the situation, and even crushed his playful spirit. So many times, I need to lighten up and take time to notice the difference between light-hearted fun and deep-seated disobedience or disrespect.

God gifted our children to us for many reasons. God gets great joy from his own children. His Word tells us, "I have no greater joy than to hear that my children are walking in the truth" (3 John 4).

Similarly, our children can be a source of great joy for us as parents. Absolutely, put the work in while they are young. Teach them, discipline them, guide them, help them learn to walk in truth. But also, enjoy them. There are so many ordinary enjoyable moments God gives us. In the face of so much heartache and sadness in our world, we have the beautiful privilege of making a lasting impression on our children.

I want Tucker to believe with all his heart that I have enjoyed him, that he has been a delight to my life. I want him to know that even after hard days, busy days, and days filled with algebra and stinky dogs, we can still laugh together. I want him to know that he is worth knowing and loving. And sometimes, these lessons are learned over snacks and drum concerts in the kitchen at midnight.

After years of living in fear and defeat, **GINA STINSON** is reclaiming every day for God's glory. She's a pastor's wife of thirty years and mom of two young adults. Gina is a storyteller writer who enjoys retelling wonderful ways God is at work. She's incredibly easy to locate on social media or at **ginastinson.com**. Otherwise, you'll find her at the hobby shop wandering the yarn aisle looking for inspiration for her next project.

Holey Socks, Holy Work

Michelle Rayburn

I GLANCED ACROSS THE LIVING ROOM to where my teenager's heels rested on the footrest of the recliner. One black sock. One sock that used to be white but was now that dingy shade they seemed to turn as soon I opened a new package of socks. It's as if they oxidize the moment the air hits them! The socks matched in the same way all of his socks coordinated: the Swiss-cheese pattern of holes laced across the bottom.

Didn't I just give him new socks? Where are they? Is it possible his socks actually smell like Swiss cheese? No. Limburger. It has holes too.

There were times when I'd wondered what purpose those socks served at all. A few threads kept the remaining patches of cloth together on his foot, and his nearly bare toes had nothing but strings between them.

It's been more than a dozen years since Dallas's holey socks roamed the halls of our home daily—or roamed the yard without shoes, which explained the holes. His old bedroom no longer smells like dirty clothes left under a bed or piled in the closet for too long without laundering. His mementos and trinkets have mostly left our storage crannies for ones in his own basement, in the home where *he* pays the mortgage.

His younger brother, Austin, had his own personal fashion trends as a teen. He had the ability to burn out a brand-new pair of tennis shoes on one five-day trip to Colorado. I don't know what happened in the mountains there, but some footwear cannot withstand the altitude, apparently. It's as if they exploded on several sides in an act of spontaneous combustion.

Austin's signature scent was, and still is, a blend of gasoline and oil—with an occasional spritz of Bondo or paint thinner. Hours of puttering in the workshop with Phil had a way of grinding that grease right into the fibers of the denim, and no amount of washing with our generic laundry detergent could do a thing about the lingering stains or odor. His room was an extension of the *eau de garage* blended with the same ripe laundry aroma his brother's room had.

Celebrating Their Differences

I came to appreciate the difference between my two boys most when they were teens. Their distinctive fragrances and fashion testified to the uniqueness of their personalities.

I came to appreciate the difference between my two boys most when they were teens. Their distinctive fragrances and fashion testified to the uniqueness of their personalities.

As soon as Austin was old enough to go over to the workshop with Phil, he dug right in with wrenches and tools, learning how to tear apart a motorcycle engine or fix a lawnmower long before he was old enough to operate one. He was the one who was there when Phil caught his hand on a fishhook buried in the carpet in the back of the Jeep and handed tools so Phil could cut away enough fibers to return home to do self-surgery on the fleshy part of his hand to remove it. If we'd had smartphones then, I'd surely have had a picture of the fuzzy mess on Phil's palm.

Dallas wanted to learn more about fixing cars, so he went to the shop too. But he brought along a book, or a notepad, or later a laptop—just in case he got bored. It never took long for him to end up *inside* the vehicle Phil and Austin had up on the hoist, windows rolled down, feet kicked up on the seat, a book or a pen in hand. Or he'd sit in the old office chair in the shop and tap away on the laptop keys while the other two tried yet another way to get a motor started. He caught pieces of the garage camaraderie that way, but he did admit to me that he found that work boring.

On other days, Dallas chose to stay home and work on homework or hobbies—sometimes from the recliner. Whether it was journaling or working, writing a fiction story, or organizing his list of books, he had to suffer through my pastime of watching Hallmark movies while I folded laundry or did housework. Sometimes we both had our laptops out while we worked on our own projects.

He often teased me with questions along these lines: "Is this the one where the girl runs into the hometown guy from high school who is *so* much better than the snobby rich lawyer she's engaged to? Or is this the widower with a daughter who meets a girl who is a writer or radio personality? Or maybe the widow with a son who meets a soldier and is surprised she's falling for another soldier? Or are the guy and girl bitter enemies in a bakeoff or decorating contest but then find true love and cooperate with each other to win it all?"

Finding Common Ground

Dallas and Austin weren't as different as night and day, as some siblings are. They actually had a lot in common as teens. I see a lot of both Phil and me in them. They both played trombone, sang in choir, and learned to play piano, following after my musical side of the family. They understood each other's inside jokes, liked similar movies, and shared some of the same friends.

They have a unique combination of Phil's calm and steady patience and my creative bent. Both did well in school—got that from me. But as teens, their specific abilities and interests became increasingly evident. As Dallas's gift for writing and public speaking developed more and Austin's talent for engineering and mechanics progressed, I wanted to nurture their gifts. However, this is difficult for us as parents if our hobbies and interests don't align with theirs.

As a fellow word-lover, it was natural for me to show an interest in Dallas's hobbies. We could talk for hours about grammar, creative writing, and books. It was more work to show an interest in Austin's motorcycle hobby, and I had no desire to understand how to fix a carburetor. Still, we found common ground in woodworking projects and design. He created a metal sculpture from repurposed gears that resonated with my repurposing hobby.

As moms of teen boys, we'll find they have some interests we don't care about at all. They'll start explaining something, and we'll try our best not to yawn or look at our watches. But we can honor their love for something even if we don't love it. We can ask good follow-up questions. Appreciate how their faces light up when they talk about favorite things. Acknowledge why it brings them joy. Celebrate how God is helping them use the abilities he gifted them with from birth. We can marvel when God leads them to a career that does just that!

> We can honor their love for something even if we don't love it.

Spoiler alert on my sons: Dallas became a high school English teacher (working with words), and Austin became a high school technology education teacher (working with auto mechanics, woodworking, robotics, and engineering).

Our work is holy work, moms. Our sons come with distinct challenges, along with their different personalities. But God designed them that way too.

Pursuing Holy Work

We don't know the impact of our work in the holey sock moments. We see ripped jeans and tattered t-shirts. We smell whatever wafts from their end of the hall. We pay the grocery bills, sit in the stands and cheer even if our son sits the bench for most of the game, listen to the marching band play the roughest rendition of "Eye of the Tiger" ever performed. We wipe pee off the floor and the toilet seat—again.

The holy work happens quietly. The aroma is subtle. We don't see the returns when it's all we can do to get through the know-it-all phase where parents are stupid. Or when teens hate us for installing a camera monitoring system from the auto insurance company into their vehicle.

Our homes are the holy ground where God is at work.

In those moments, God knows. He sees every time you validate your son's uniqueness. When you support his hobbies that are nothing like yours, or when they are just like yours. Our homes are the holy ground where God is at work.

This is where he works out fruit in our own lives, not just for our sons. As we learn to apply love and patience, God brings grace. Sometimes moms need do-overs too. In the apologies, kindness and gentleness grow. From our own self-control, a second generation learns. Joy, peace, goodness, and faithfulness are sacred gifts with everlasting value that spring up in tender hearts, even in hard places.

Success is not raising perfect children. It's in giving of ourselves and depending on our perfect God in the whole process. Holiness is there in the holey sock moments that are sure to show up somewhere every day.

MICHELLE RAYBURN is an author and podcast host who helps others find hope in the trashy stuff of life. She has an MA in ministry leadership and writes Christian living books, humor, and Bible studies. Together with her husband, they've raised two sons and gained two daughters-in-law—plus three granddaughters (go estrogen team!) and a grandson. Dark chocolate, an iced coffee, and a good book in the hammock top Michelle's favorites list. **michellerayburn.com**

Young Men

Short Time, Far-Reaching Influence

Rhonda Stoppe

IF YOU DIDN'T KNOW HIM, you might have thought, *This kid has it all together!* Tony was a handsome young man with beautiful blue eyes and a smile that lit up the room. He was student body president, a high school football quarterback, and had a 4.0 grade point average. What's not to love, right?

God did not bring our oldest son, Tony, into our lives until he was fifteen years old. He was in our youth group, where my husband served as youth pastor. Learning about his troubled home life broke our hearts. But we also observed how God used his circumstances to bring Tony to Jesus. Watching Tony be drawn to Christ was a joy to behold. After Tony surrendered his heart to Jesus, our relationship with him grew closer. Soon, Tony began to unfold details of his difficult childhood. I am not at liberty to share, but we soon realized that his over-achieving tendencies were his coping response.

Through a series of painful circumstances, Tony found himself without a place to call home—and in desperate need of a family. The Lord began tugging at my heart. In the fifteen years my husband had been a youth pastor, we had met countless teens who needed to be rescued. But somehow, *this* teen, *this* boy, was special. He was *our* boy. He was the one God would call us to raise as our own.

But somehow, *this* teen, *this* boy, was special. He was *our* boy. He was the one God would call us to raise as our own.

Accepting the Brevity

Tony lived in our home for a short season until he went away to college. But just as the Lord had used Jochebed's few years with her son Moses to shape him for life, God gave us a brief window of opportunity to give Tony a strong godly foundation.

If you're not familiar with Jochebed's account in Scripture, you can find it in Exodus 2:1–10. Here is a breakdown of the story. During Israel's enslavement in Egypt, Jochebed gave birth to her son Moses. And, because the Pharaoh was concerned that the Israelites might one day outnumber and overpower them, he decreed that all baby boys should be put to death. After hiding her son for three months, God put into Jochebed's heart to send sweet Moses down the Nile River in nothing more than a handmade basket that she lined with pitch to keep out the water.

Here is how the Bible describes Jochebed's plight: "But when she could no longer hide him, she got a basket made of papyrus reeds and waterproofed it with tar and pitch. She put the baby in the basket and laid it among the reeds along the bank of the Nile River" (Exodus 2:3).

I shudder to think of how Jochebed must have felt while she watched her little baby float away from her protection and into the unknown. But God knew. He sent Moses into the very arms of Pharaoh's daughter, who would adopt him as her own son. And here's the cool part. God sovereignly allowed Jochebed to become Moses's nursemaid. So, for the few years Jochebed nursed her boy, she would have had opportunity to teach him about the one true God of Israel.

God used Jochebed's few years with Moses to imprint upon his heart and mind a biblical worldview and truth that would help him withstand the Egyptians' teachings of idol worship. "Her teachings were likely the foundation God used to build Moses's faith."[11]

Imagine how hard it would have been for Jochebed, who eventually had to leave her sweet son in the care of a woman who practiced a pagan religion! I know some moms who agonize over leaving their son for the weekend with an ungodly stepmother. Maybe you can relate?

Redeeming the Time

Are you, like me, the mother of an adopted son? Or perhaps you are a foster mother or stepmom. Have you wondered if your time with your son will make any sort of an impact? You're not alone. I've been in your shoes.

When I became Tony's mom, I often thought, *Will this season in our home really make a difference? Is there time to help him understand his worth? Would a few short years be enough to influence our boy with a biblical worldview?*

I made every effort to connect with Tony during his brief time with us. I wanted to sit him down and teach him all the things, but I knew that was not the most effective way to win his heart or inspire him to listen.

Rather, Tony had an old Jeep that he would work on in our driveway at night. It was more pleasant to do automotive work after dark because Texas weather is so hot.

After I tucked our two younger children into bed, I would sit in the Jeep while Tony worked on the engine. It was a convertible, so it was easy to have conversations with him while his head was under the hood.

Men communicate well shoulder-to-shoulder, so these chats in the Jeep provided the perfect opportunity to connect with Tony in a way

---

11. Rhonda Stoppe, *Moms Raising Sons to Be Men* (Eugene, OR: Harvest House Publishers, 2023), 26.

that didn't intimidate him or make him feel as if I were trying to force a conversation.

On those hot summer nights, Tony and I had great talks about his new life as a believer, and we talked about girls. We talked about his dream to become a fighter pilot, about God's character, and about girls. We discussed God's plan for marriage . . . and did I mention we talked about girls?

I am certain if I had seated Tony in my kitchen and said, "Let's talk about girls," he would not have spoken so freely and openly as he did while working on his Jeep.

Being a Momma

Over the years, Tony related to me with love and respect—but never as his momma. I wanted to be a mom to him, but I honored that he had a mother whom he loved, so he didn't necessarily think he needed another.

Upon graduating from high school as class valedictorian, Tony was accepted to Texas A&M University.

Right away, Tony, our overachiever, went out for the A&M drill team, a much sought-after and competitive position. The requirements were grueling. All the while, he was taking a full load of classes and participating in ROTC life. By September, Tony had been selected for the team, and he was thrilled—thrilled and exhausted.

> He had been such a man and accomplished great things. Now all I could hear was a little boy who needed a mother.

One day, Tony called home. In a weak and shaky voice, he said he had a severe case of pneumonia and would need to take a break from all activities. He told me he was not going to tell his drill commander he was sick for fear of losing his place on the team. Oh, my sweet boy who had worked so hard to achieve his goals! He had been such a man and accomplished great things. Now all I could hear was a little boy who needed a mother.

I asked the Lord for discernment. We as mothers need to learn when God wants us to step back and allow our young men to battle their trials alone and when he would have us offer to intervene. Somehow, I sensed this was one of those intervening times. Tony had worked so hard to land a spot on the team, and now he was terribly sick. I felt that the least I could do was ask Tony if I could make a phone call on his behalf. Reluctantly, he agreed. I reached out to a friend of Tony's who was an alumnus of the school. He promised to make some calls.

Soon I heard back from the drill team's commander, who called to assure me that my son's place on the team was secure. With that taken care of, we drove several hours to bring our very sick boy home, where I took care of him until he got better.

Embracing the Trials

With the concern of a mother, I spent almost two weeks nursing Tony back to health. Through that experience, God knit our hearts together, and I became a momma to Tony.[12]

Sometimes God allows or—dare I say—"sends" trials in the lives of our sons to do a work we know nothing about. While at the time, it seemed unfair for Tony's illness to jeopardize his position on the drill team, looking back, we can see how God divinely orchestrated Tony's frailty to show him what it's like to be cared for by his family. And how to be nurtured and loved by me—his momma.

Living the Dream

Tony went on to graduate from college and became an F-22 fighter pilot. While he has achieved many amazing goals, I was never more proud of him than on the day he called to say, "You know, I am living my dream, and I now realize that it is not enough. My Sunday school teacher, a retired fighter pilot, told me that if I am doing all of this but I'm not surrendered to Christ, my life will be wasted."

---

12. *Moms Raising Sons to Be Men*, 26–27

Tony retired from the Air Force as a lieutenant colonel. He is married to Kylene, the sweetest southern girl who loves Jesus. They have two precious children who they are teaching to follow Christ. Both Tony and Kylene serve in a ministry that supports children from troubled homes. They bring their own children with them each week to minister at a homeless encampment. And when their children ask why, they tell them the story of how Tony, a young boy in need of a family, became our son.

MOMMA, DON'T MINIMIZE THE SHORT season you are allowed to nurture an adopted, foster, or stepson. And don't get stuck in regret over not having more time with him. The Lord's timing is perfect. His ways are above our ways. In whatever time the Lord affords, he invites you to influence your son—and his generation—by faithfully teaching him truth.

What an amazing ministry of motherhood God has given to you and me. We are the vessels that the Lord will use to nurture our son and teach him God's ways.

When asked how being a part of our family influenced him, Tony said, "The family was, and continues to be, my living definition of both what God expects from me, and what He wants for me. I am thankful for this example, and I have no doubt that it was God's plan for our lives to connect."[13]

RHONDA STOPPE is a popular speaker, best-selling author of seven books, podcast host of *Old Ladies Know Stuff*, and international media personality. Rhonda was named in the "best of episode" at Focus on the Family. The Stoppes have four children and fifteen grandchildren. For free resources, or to book Rhonda to speak at your event please visit: **NoRegretsWoman.com**.

13. *Moms Raising Sons to Be Men*, 28.

A Sparkling Surprise for a Single Mom

Christina Ryan Claypool

RAISING A CHILD ALONE, I discovered what should have been the most festive season was often the greatest reminder of the absence of family in the traditional sense. Our modest yuletide celebrations didn't bear any resemblance to the sentimental TV commercials where loved ones gather around a large dining table—decorated with a poinsettia centerpiece and flickering candles—laden with delicious, steaming dishes. A scene where holiday music plays softly in the background. Ours probably looked more like Bob Cratchit's meager, although joyful celebration depicted in Charles Dickens's classic novel, *A Christmas Carol.*

Treasured Traditions

On Christmas Eve, it was usually just Zach and me because my mother, stepfather, and most of our other relatives lived out of state. Despite this, when Zachary was young, I tried desperately to achieve some sense of Christmas cheer while operating within a confining budget. I never expected any presents. Like many solo parents, I only cared that there would be something special under the tree for my precious youngster. Even the Christmas tree in our apartment was a hand-me-down from another once-single mom who had remarried and graduated to improved economic security.

Still, at Christmastime, I did my best to make sure there were lots of packages for Zach to open. Not expensive items, just tiny tokens of how grateful I was to have been granted the privilege of raising him. My sensitive dark-haired boy never expected much or complained there should have been more. He understood our "situation."

My sensitive dark-haired boy never expected much or complained there should have been more. He understood our "situation."

Well, except for the year when he was three or four and desperately wanted a specific toy I couldn't buy for him. It wasn't an extremely expensive item. Rather, it was a widely popular plastic car that was out of stock everywhere. It certainly wasn't a very merry Christmas, tainted by my then toddler's tantrum and tears. It might have been the Christmas Zach first decided it was best not to desire material goods since it was distressful and disappointing when those expectations were left unmet.

Every single parent's story is probably complicated because real life can be messy. In my case, Zachary's father and I were married only briefly and for all the wrong reasons. Following our divorce mere months after our infant son was born, his dad moved back in with his parents. Yet Zach's now late father always made sure his little boy had an impressive gift. However, the present usually remained at his dad's house awaiting their weekend visits. I wanted Zach to have toys and dreamed-of items at our apartment where he could enjoy them daily.

Bountiful Blessings

There's a famous quote from Jesus in an age-old Bible verse that represents the plight of the single-parent family best: "'It is more blessed to give than to receive'" (Acts 20:35). You have to learn to give without expectation because frequently, little comes back. On a positive note, this serves as a reminder that the true meaning of Christmas was never about gifts. Instead, it was about a tiny baby born in Bethlehem sent to save our lost world.

Of course, there were benevolent family members and friends from work or church who realized our circumstances were financially challenging. Sometimes, little blessings such as an unexpected gift certificate, a toy for Zach wrapped in colorful paper, or a Christmas sweater for me appeared during the holidays.

At other times, folks got consumed with their own families, and the season seemed bleak and lonely. It was then I tried to muster a cheerful face for my boy, who recognized things were not the way they were supposed to be. So, it was for most of those first twenty Christmases my son and I spent together. Along the way, he became an independent young man, moved out, and began a life of his own.

I tried to muster a cheerful face for my boy, who recognized things were not the way they were supposed to be.

New Norms

When Christmas Eve rolled around the year he was almost twenty, Zach arrived at my door to celebrate our tradition of enjoying the evening together. There was the usual church service, a tree with twinkling lights, and a modest feast.

Yet there was also a new person joining us for our celebration. Larry Claypool, a public school administrator and never-married bachelor, who was patiently trying to discover the key to my closed-off heart and slowly winning my son over as well.

Although a couple of months earlier, Larry and I were driving home after having a fun day away when he brought up the possibility of marriage in our future. "Never mention the subject again, or our relationship will be over," I answered frantically.

Larry's face clouded with confusion, not understanding my response wasn't about him. It was about my past heartbreak. I was trapped by fear, terrified of being hurt again. Still, the forty-eight-year-old bachelor had become a stable presence in our lives, and celebrating our first Christmas together felt right.

After a candlelight church service, we returned to my apartment to open presents. When Zach finished unwrapping his gifts, his face radiated with excitement as he proudly handed me a small box. I began to tear the decorative paper, expecting a pair of costume earrings or gold-plated bracelet like in years past. His eyes, eager with anticipation, focused intently on me.

Generous Gift

Lifting the lid of the ivory satin case, I tried to hide my shock. It bore the name of an expensive jewelry store. I could barely swallow an audible gasp when I glanced down and saw a diamond pendant and glittering chain resting in the box's burgundy velvet lining. By now, Zach's deep blue eyes were dancing with unrestrained delight. Apparently, my son understood the importance of giving.

Unfortunately, I had not discovered how to graciously receive because I'd had little practice. *How much had this necklace cost him?* It looked to be at least a quarter-carat diamond circled by a thick band of white gold. The unmistakable sparkle of the stone left little doubt that it was real, and Zach's ecstatic look confirmed its authenticity.

The delicate pendant was exquisite, but my faithful man-child worked hard for his retail salary and was attending college too. I often felt guilty that I couldn't financially assist him more in achieving his educational and career goals.

Priceless Presents

I thought about the Christmas sermon from the year before. Pastor David Sharpes had spoken about accepting gifts with appreciation and graciousness, never offending the giver regardless of what the gift was.

It hadn't been challenging that Christmas Eve; my son had given me a small handmade boat made of plywood filled with a few biblical characters and painted animals a couple inches tall. Understanding how significant Old Testament stories are to me, Zach bought the facsimile set of ancient Noah, who had built an ark to survive a catastrophic flood. The miniature wooden set was adorable, but it wasn't extravagant or expensive—it came from an affordable local shop. In contrast, staring at the finely crafted necklace, I was faced with accepting something that seemed too much.

Zach began telling the story of the gift's origin, a tender tale about a co-worker his age who was a single mom with a little boy. Needing extra cash, she was selling the diamond pendant. This gift from a former boyfriend didn't possess any sentimental value. Zach had simply purchased it to help her make ends meet and to bless me with an incredible Christmas present.

My gift was a visible witness that he had learned the most valuable lesson the holidays can teach. It truly *is* more blessed to give than to receive.

Suddenly, the diamond sparkled brighter, and I looked at the glistening gold necklace with new appreciation. Instantly, I realized Zachary had seen our lives and struggles replicated in the life of a fellow employee who was also a college student like I had been when he was just a toddler. My gift was a visible witness that he had learned the most valuable lesson the holidays can teach. It truly *is* more blessed to give than to receive.

Larry sat quietly as Zach and I shared this intimate moment between a single mother and her adult child. Not one to give up, though, not long after, my gentle suitor asked my son if he could have his permission to marry me. Zach's reply took me by surprise when he told Larry he needed his support too. This sort of cinched the deal.

By Valentines Day, I owned another diamond in the form of a sparkling engagement ring. That June, we became a family of three, now keeping our annual Christmas tradition quite similar to the very first one together.

Still, I doubt there could ever be another present under the tree able to match how blessed I felt the Christmas when I received the diamond necklace from my beloved boy. After all, even though your son grows up to be a good man, one you are immensely proud of, in a mother's heart, he will always be your little boy.

CHRISTINA RYAN CLAYPOOL is a former reporter/producer for WTLW TV 44, an award-winning past newspaper columnist, six-time *Chicken Soup for the Soul* book contributor, and author of several Christian books, including *Secrets of the Pastor's Wife: A Novel.* She has been featured on CBN's 700 Club and Joyce Meyer Ministries TV show. Christina graduated from Bluffton University and also earned a master of arts in ministry from Mount Vernon Nazarene University. Learn more at **christinaryanclaypool.com**.

The Winking Elvis and a Type A Soldier

Kim Cusimano

ONE OF THE BIGGEST DELIGHTS and surprises over the years is parenting children who are so different from each other. Our two sons are no exception. Today, one is on his first Navy deployment in Europe. The other works part-time at Whataburger and has a hobby of being an Elvis tribute artist. That should be enough to tell you I had a range of parenting experiences raising two boys, and no parenting book in those early years covered such topics as how to raise Elvis.

In this new season of having young adult children, I am enjoying the opportunity to reflect on those early years of parenting. I was not just raising sons, but I was raising boys to be men. In their young years, I knew this, but it was hard not to be consumed with the practical things of their childhood. There were school lunches to pack, field trips, sporting events, school plays, church youth group, and everything that comes with raising children.

Embrace the Differences

One of my sons had a way of running the mower into the fence or over huge tree roots. At the time, I thought I should be concerned about how he would eventually drive a car. This is the same son that now steers a U.S. naval ship. I think it's good that God didn't give me a peek into his future. I guess the U.S. Navy should thank us that at least we thought to have him practice driving a riding mower when he was fifteen.

Isn't that crazy, though? See the gap in what I thought I knew? I worried about him driving a car and didn't have enough sense to worry about him driving a ship! And how about the time warp? How did all that progression happen so fast? The time between driving the lawn mower and the billion-dollar ship?

As moms, we can have dreams for our sons, but they will certainly have their own.

My son Ben taught me many things, but some specific ones come to mind. First, as moms, we can have dreams for our sons, but they will certainly have their own. It was a process over years of learning to support, highlight, and honor his strengths, goals, and ambitions. Sometimes it meant laying down my ideas for him. There was that time I put him in gymnastics, but it wasn't a great fit, or the bowl haircut that was my idea and not his. But hey, it grew out! He can stop bringing it up whenever he sees his five-year-old self in pictures. I got the message. It wasn't my best work.

Second, I learned there is a difference between guiding and controlling. Ben was a natural leader, a driven, type A personality even as a young boy. I started to recognize a facial expression of hurt if I was trying to control his ideas. If he sensed I didn't trust his decisions, ideas, or abilities, even if he seemed angry, I learned hurt was most often the underlying emotion. God had wired him for independence and leadership.

As moms, just like that time warp that moved Ben from the lawnmower to the ship, one day, we are controlling what our toddler son eats, wears, and does. In what seems like the very next minute, they have a profound need to feel respected, intelligent, and capable. We must adjust on the fly, but don't worry; God has equipped us. Don't forget you are the same person who can start dinner, put in a load of laundry, decorate the birthday cupcakes, and sell eight hundred tins of Boy Scout popcorn on your social media page, all within thirty minutes.

Sometimes we need to use these same skill sets in unexpected ways. God made us agile and flexible. I promise you will keep up with the fast-moving changes. Some days you will feel your son is outpacing you, but when he hugs you on his graduation day, you will know you made the transitions when needed. That cap, gown, and tassel will remind you that you gave him space to grow up. And, like me, along the way, you pray, trust God, and ask him for help. Two verses that came to mind often were Proverbs 3:5–6: "Trust in the LORD with all your heart; do not depend on your own understanding. Seek his will in all you do, and he will show you which path to take."

In the early years of parenting, I learned that verses such as these were not meant just to be printed on fancy frames and hung for decoration around my home but for instruction, support, and help.

I learned that verses such as these were not meant just to be printed on fancy frames and hung for decoration around my home but for instruction, support, and help.

Embrace Their Expression

And, another thing, how did I end up living with Elvis? My oldest son was born with a syndrome called C.H.A.R.G.E. that affected his heart, eyes, kidney, and overall development. For example, his right eye did not fully develop, and he had various developmental delays. As a toddler, he started wearing a prosthetic eye. He also has characteristics of autism, such as hyperfocus on things that interest him. Another important tidbit: my children are adopted from Korea. To paint the complete picture, I live with a one-eyed Korean Elvis today. You didn't see that coming, did you? Funny, I didn't either!

In his teen years, he discovered Elvis and was fascinated by his colorful clothing and larger-than-life persona. He asked for replica clothing, music, and books about Elvis for his birthday and Christmas. I thought this phase would run its course like Batman or LEGO sets. Ten years later, he still loves all things Elvis. He loves performing in his Elvis-replica jumpsuits and clothing for senior centers and other special events. For the record, a Korean, one-eyed Elvis is more convincing than you would think.

Nate, like his younger brother, Ben, helped me learn new things about parenting and supporting those around me. First, never limit, underestimate, or judge someone's unique abilities. I'm a mom to a son with differing abilities, and he amazes me daily. I don't mind being called a special needs mom, but I am humored by the fact my son has very few needs these days. He, like his brother, needs me less and less. Oh, it's true he doesn't drive or take care of his own business paperwork, such as taxes, but don't we all need support in one area or another? Cue our tax accountants and Uber drivers.

Now, looking back, my mom dreams weren't big or creative enough for him.

When Nate came home from Korea as an infant, his malformed right eye always looked like he was winking at me. Cuteness was his trump card. Wrapped in all that cuteness were God's plans and purpose for him. Now, looking back, my mom dreams weren't big or creative enough for him.

This leads me to the next important lesson he taught me: I worried too much. I worried more about what he couldn't do or might not be able to do than what he could. In the early years, I worried if he would learn to read. When he did learn to read, I worried if he could read fast enough to keep up with other kids. There was always the next skill to worry about. I also worried about his social development. Would he fit in? Would he have friends?

There were many concerns and challenging days in the mix, but looking back, he was more like other children than not, and my worries were actually similar to my concerns for my other children. If you are a mom to a differing-abilities child, I'm near sure it would be a waste of paper and ink to tell you not to worry, but I challenge you to never worry about your child's future apart from hope. Don't let worry or fear steal away joy, hope, and big dreams.

> God is in the business of doing more than we ever expected.

Hope is a great escort for the beautiful things to come. Don't be afraid to dream big things for your child. I was always encouraged when I read Ephesians 3:20: "Now all glory to God, who is able, through his mighty power to work within us, to accomplish infinitely more than we might ask or think." Chances are, like me, you will look back one day and realize you didn't dream big enough. God is in the business of doing more than we ever expected.

Embrace the Joy

I didn't know years ago what I didn't know, and you know what? It all worked out. It worked out better and was more exciting than I could have ever expected. I am so proud of my son's Navy service; he looks dashing in that uniform. And you guessed it. That type A personality with natural leadership skills perfectly fits his job and career field. There is such joy in seeing it all come together in his young adult years.

When his oldest brother puts on that Elvis jumpsuit and those sweet older ladies at the senior centers start cheering, waving their arms, and grinning the biggest grin, I cry. I think I choke up every time he performs. The joy he brings others when he performs is palpable in the room. And let me note here that the red, burning love Elvis jumpsuit can stand toe to toe with the U.S. Navy uniform. Add two handsome sons, and both can take my breath away!

Embrace God's Plans

Our two sons are so different from one another. Their strengths, skills, and careers are different. They know and influence different people. It reminds me that God's designs, plans, and purposes are more than I could have known. One of my favorite passages that reflects this is Isaiah 55:8–9. "'My thoughts are nothing like your thoughts,' says the Lord. 'And my ways are far beyond anything you could imagine. For just as the heavens are higher than the earth, so my ways are higher than your ways and my thoughts higher than your thoughts.'" His ways have been beyond anything I could imagine and so much better.

I am grateful to God for my sons, and that on the parenting journey, he grew me and drew me to himself. It has been a win-win! I have two treasured sons, now young men, and a deeper, more intimate relationship with God. Moms to young sons, hang in there. You are in for some big wins of your own!

KIM CUSIMANO is a wife and mother to four. She writes to encourage special needs families and long-term caregivers. Kim and her husband like to think of themselves as hybrid empty nesters. They have launched two young adults and have two special needs young adults in their home. Parenting young children and navigating the school years are behind them. They are enjoying finding new adventures as a party of four! Visit Kim at **fulljoyministries.com**.

Forgiveness Sets Us Free

Maureen Miller

YOU NEED TO ASK FORGIVENESS. That's what the Holy Spirit whispered to my heart as I sat in Asbury University's Hughes Auditorium that chilly February night. My twenty-three-year-old son Isaac* stood behind me, his arms crossed. His girlfriend sat several seats away, her head in her hands.

My heart pounded. *Really, God?*

Had I heard him correctly? The incidents flashed before my eyes—indiscretions that had mostly occurred many years prior when our middle child was a toddler. As a boy. And a teenager.

But as the worship music continued, hundreds of young men and women with arms outstretched in praise, I knew. I'd heard God loud and clear.

We returned from that visit to our alma mater with renewed hope. It had been a miracle we'd even gotten into the main building where this awakening began on February 8, 2023, with Isaac his girlfriend, and our thirteen-year-old daughter. We prayed the seeds planted would grow. Bear fruit.

And me? I returned home with a challenge.

Potty Training Our Three-Year-Old

"Isaac, what have you done?" My face had flushed with hot anger.

My toddler's lips puckered, but he refused to cry as I swatted his bottom. He retreated to his room where his toys were spread out on the floor, and I closed the bathroom door.

Help me, Lord. My chest pounded, and I sensed the pulsing of blood in my head as it kept time with the beat of my heart. Taking a deep breath, I exhaled. *Please help me know how to help him. I'm failing as a mother, and I hate when I lose my patience.*

After months of potty training, when I'd make Isaac sit on the potty often and for long periods of time, only for him to have an accident the moment his pants were back up, I was at a loss.

And the Enemy sneered, *You're a terrible mother. You're destroying your son, and he's not even out of pull-ups.*

Truth is, I felt that way. My reaction, much of the time, was frustration rather than quiet patience, and I feared Isaac would grow bitter.

My reaction, much of the time, was frustration rather than quiet patience.

Homeschooling a Sleepyhead

"For the hundredth time, get up." I shook our ten-year-old, whose slender body was still cocooned in bedclothes. "This is your last warning!"

We battled often, Isaac and me. With he not being a morning person, rousing him for school stirred my frustration and left me feeling drained, despite that second cup of coffee.

No matter how I threatened, how loud my voice grew, it took prodding and poking—even pouring cold water once—to get Isaac downstairs to start his school day.

Please help me, Lord, I often prayed before my feet hit the floor.

The tension between us some mornings was thick and cold, like day-old oatmeal, and my heart was often heavy with the strain. Our personalities were different in more ways than one. Though we'd had Isaac since birth, had the blessing of years of parenting him, he struggled to adapt to our homeschooling schedule after having several years in public school. Perhaps it was the lack of peer involvement, and though he and his older brother loved one another, they, too, were quite different in disposition.

Despite our differences, we plodded through—somehow managing to achieve success.

Still, despite our differences, we plodded through—somehow managing to achieve success in our boys' education for a number of years until our oldest graduated and Isaac attended a charter school for his last two years of high school.

But I worried about him—perceived he was struggling inside, though I didn't know exactly how to help him.

Again, Satan would hiss, *You failed as his teacher when he was a potty-training-toddler, and you're still failing. What a loser!*

Being a Poor Listener

"Mom, watch this funny video." Isaac, now seventeen, laid the iPad on the kitchen counter where I was cutting vegetables for dinner.

"How long is it?" Not wanting to be interrupted at that moment, a surge of annoyance reflected in my voice as I wiped my hands on my jeans.

Undeterred, he hit play. "Just a couple minutes." And he laughed, knowing what was coming, excited for me to share in the humor.

We watched, and I laughed too—the male stand-up comedian imitating pulling on yoga pants, fumbling around on the stage, his face contorting almost beyond recognition.

"Wasn't that funny?" Isaac swiped tears. "And wait, here's one more."

Before he could hit play again, however, I interrupted the moment. "No. Not now, Isaac. Maybe later. I need to finish dinner."

My son sort of humphed but conceded. "Okay. Later." Turning to leave the kitchen, he said, "But wasn't that funny, Mom? I knew you'd think so."

As I picked up the knife to continue chopping carrots, I heard once more the voice of the Enemy. *You never have enough time for him. You're impatient and unkind, thwarting his joy.*

And though I recognized it was Satan again, knew his snide accusations weren't true, his words pierced. Reality was, our tech-savvy son always had something to show me on his iPad, and I struggled. So often, even if I had time to spare, I'd only give him half my attention if I listened at all, and I'd be left wondering later what it was he had actually said.

I knew God would offer guidance while the Enemy would only continue his assaults.

Why can't I be a better listener? It was both a prayer and a complaint—though I knew God would offer guidance while the Enemy would only continue his assaults.

And as the years went by, Isaac graduated from high school, moved out to live nearer his work at a lumber company, and I still struggled sometimes to be a good listener. To really lean in and give him my undivided attention.

Pursuing Forgiveness

You need to ask forgiveness. The words the Holy Spirit spoke to me. I looked over my shoulder to see my now adult son standing back against the wall, arms crossed.

The worship of hundreds of people in Hughes was mostly gentle but would rise and, like a wave, stir shouts of praise and applause throughout the auditorium that late February night. Was Isaac moved? I couldn't tell.

Father, help me know how to reach him. He seems so far, and I'm afraid I'm somehow to blame.

Never accusing, the conviction of the Holy Spirit is kind though persistent. I heard again, *You need to ask forgiveness.*

Never accusing, the conviction of the Holy Spirit is kind though persistent.

Several weeks after our return from Asbury University, where the revival stirred and then spread to other college and university campuses, I dialed my son's number.

"Lord, help me," I whispered as I waited, half hoping he wouldn't answer.

"Hey, Mom." His voice was cheerful, and I could hear music in the background.

"You driving? I can call back."

"No, it's fine. I'm on lunch break, just sitting here eatin' a sub."

"Well, I was thinking of you." I paused, took a deep breath. "Um, if you have a minute, I wanted to tell you something."

"Sure. Yeah, it's a good time. What's up?"

My heart pounded. "I wanted to . . ." Again, a pause. "I want to ask your forgiveness, Son. I know in my heart I need to say I'm sorry for—" My voice broke.

"What is it, Mom?"

"While we were at Asbury a few weeks ago, while we were worshipping, I heard the Lord say I needed to tell you I'm sorry for some things."

Isaac, always the jokester, replied, "Oh no. You already apologized for killing Beta Fish Bob. Remember? I forgave you long ago."

It was my turn to chuckle, and it felt good. My heart slowed a bit. "Well, I did feel really bad about that. Poor guy, but no. Not that." Again, I took a deep breath. "I'm asking you to forgive me for the times I lashed out in anger—spanked you when I was frustrated, mostly during potty training. That was wrong, and I'm so sorry."

Another breath, then, "And I also want to apologize for how impatient I'd get when you were young and we'd battle it out over school. I didn't always handle my frustration very well, and I'm sorry for that."

Isaac was quiet, apparently waiting to see if I was finished.

"And one more thing. I haven't always been a good listener. Even now, I sometimes struggle. When you were a teenager, especially, and you'd want to show me videos and memes, and my head would spin." I stopped, swallowing rising emotion. "I know now that you were just trying to share with me more of what you enjoyed, and I was too often impatient. Frankly, I missed lots of opportunities to bond that way, and I'm so sorry."

Isaac didn't say anything immediately. Finally, "Mom, it's okay. Honest. I don't even remember much of what you just described. Really. You're a great mom, and I forgive you." It was his turn to pause, take a breath, before concluding, "I love you, Mom."

Finding Freedom in Forgiveness

Tears fell as I received his words, hearing them in both my head *and* in my heart. "I love you too, Son," I choked. "And I'm thankful for you and your presence in our lives. You bring so much to our family, and we're proud of you."

And it's true. Isaac, with his unique personality, his wit, and—yes!—his tech-infused wisdom (he knows all things YouTube) is a wonderful son.

As the scripture says, "Love prospers when a fault is forgiven" (Proverbs 17:9). Indeed, love won when I said I was sorry to my son.

Not only was Isaac perhaps freed for further growth that only the Holy Spirit can do, but his mom was too. Yes, I was set free—finally healed from years of inner hurt that came from believing the lies of the Enemy.

Truth is, God's grace covered each of my shortcomings when I cried out to him.

And Isaac?

He thinks—has always thought—I'm a good mother, something I only fully discovered when I asked for forgiveness, heard him say it: "I love you, Mom."

And that's why saying "Forgive me" sets us free. Know why?

Because love *always* wins!

*Name changed.

MAUREEN MILLER is an award-winning author who is a contributing writer for *Guideposts* and several online devotional websites, and she writes regularly for her local newspaper. She loves life in all its forms and enjoys it with her husband, their three children and their grandchildren on Selah Farm, their hobby homestead in western North Carolina. She blogs at **penningpansies.com**, sharing stories of God's extraordinary character in the ordinary things of life.

Learners and Leaders Who Love God

Pam Farrel

I WAS ROCKING OUR NEWBORN SON, Brock, feeling very overwhelmed at the prospect of raising a boy through to adulthood. I prayed, "Lord, we are in youth work, and it seems some kids soar and succeed while others falter and fall. What is the difference?"

I made a list of all the leadership qualities I saw in the most successful teens, then jotted down a list of practical skills we would need to weave into our son by the time he was eighteen. I pulled out a prayer I had written, one I wanted to frame and give when he went to college. Part of that prayer was: *God, give him the faith of a Daniel or a Joseph. Give him the courage to stand alone for you. Give him the integrity and wisdom to choose well in his relationships. Lead him to the godly woman he will marry someday.*

We decided that once a year, we would have a celebration, a "Learner and Leader Who Loves God Day."[14] On that day, we would negotiate privileges and responsibilities, and we would select one leadership trait

14. Concepts from this chapter appear in: Bill and Pam Farrel, *The 10 Best Decisions a Parent Can Make* (Eugene, Oregon: Harvest House Publishers, 2006).

from the list to focus on building into our son. We also selected a verse to pray over that boy all year. We decided to add in some Farrel family fun. To make it more like a Christmas or birthday celebration, we also gave a gift that celebrates his uniqueness. The gift had three qualities:

Practical – something already in our budget, like a lunch box, gym bag, backpack, or item we knew he might need in the coming year.

Personal – to celebrate his unique passion or calling. These things could be art supplies, musical instruments, sporting gear, a new Bible, or other item that represented who we saw God creating him to be.

Prophetic – something to speak promise about or applaud the potential strength or talent we saw God budding in our son.

Worthwhile Work

Sometimes, when we share the Learner and Leader tradition, we get a little pushback from already busy parents: "This is so intense! It feels like homework for parents! Is it worth all the time, money, and effort? Does God answer when we pray?"

Let me share a few stories. Then you decide.

Let's jump ahead about a dozen years from our eldest's first Learner and Leader Who Loves God Day. Each fall, we faithfully celebrated each son's uniqueness and gave gifts to reinforce godly living and who we observed God was creating him to be. We held to the responsibilities and privileges worksheet year after year.

Brock was a freshman in high school. He was a three-sport athlete who wanted to play sports in high school. The best athletic program in our area was the public high school. We told him, "Yes, you can go to the public high school—but your goal is to influence others to make wise decisions, and as they see God shining through you, share your faith and give them the opportunity for a friendship with Christ too."

We connected our son to the local Campus Crusade for Christ (CRU) leader and the Fellowship of Christian Athletes (FCA) representative, and Brock heartily agreed to have the CRU leader be his mentor. Brock also gathered his friends to launch an FCA Huddle at the high school.

A few months in, Brock came to us and said, "My friends have these big dreams, but to get to those dreams, I think what they really need is Jesus."

Brock and his mentor challenged us to buy pizza for the freshman football team. At the after-practice party, the athletes played icebreaker games, and the leaders gave out door prizes. Before they distributed the pizza and cookies, Brock shared his personal testimony of how he began a relationship with Christ, and then a professional football player also shared his faith story. Brock led out in prayer, giving all the players an opportunity to come to know Christ in a personal way.

Brock repeated this outreach for his basketball and volleyball teams, and by year's end, over thirty-four young men had received Christ as their Savior. Each week, either Brock or a guest speaker would lead a lunchtime Bible study (with food provided by the FCA moms and my Moms In Prayer group). By the end of our son's senior year, that FCA Huddle had almost 200 students involved.

> One of my first recorded prayer requests penned in my prayer journal was, "God, please give Brock a brave backbone! Make him courageous!"

Our son is Brock William. Brock means "badger," the most courageous of animals that will defend his home and family from predators much larger. When he was a toddler, he was very whiny, and one of my first recorded prayer requests penned in my prayer journal was, "God, please give Brock a brave backbone! Make him courageous!"

William, his middle name, means "guardian of the gospel." As we watched Brock's teen years unfold with confidence empowered by God, we marveled!

God answers prayer.

A New Thing

Some of my favorite verses to pray over our family invite the Lord to lovingly press closer into him:

> I am about to do something new.
> See, I have already begun! Do you not see it?
> I will make a pathway through the wilderness.
> I will create rivers in the dry wasteland. (Isaiah 43:19)

Fast-forward to Brock's junior year. We were at the first football game where he was to be the starting varsity quarterback. He had called up his buddies on the team and said, "This week, after the game, I'm going to the 50-yard line to pray. Will you join me?"

They all said, "We're there for you, man!"

Bill and I prayed with our son the morning of that first game. Then my Moms in Prayer group joined in praying too. That night, the team *lost* thirty-eight to zero. Discouraged, the players all just wandered off the field—all except Brock, who went straight to the 50-yard line and knelt down—all alone.

Standing near my husband, I said to Bill, "Honey, he's all alone! Should I run down and pray with him?"

My wise husband said with a bit of humor, "Oh yeah, Pam, that's what the varsity quarterback wants—his mommy running on the field!"

I remembered the prayer we had uttered years before. "Help him stand alone for you, God." And now he was.

Just then, I remembered the prayer we had uttered years before. "Help him stand alone for you, God." And now he was.

Soon, three players from the *opposing* team joined Brock, and they prayed. After the game, some of Brock's youth leaders went to encourage him. Then we made our way to the field.

I threw my arms around my son. Reaching up, I took his face in my hands and said, "I have never been more proud of you than I am at this moment. I know tonight was one of the hardest nights of your life, but you kept your word to God. Remember our family motto: 'Those who honor God, God honors.'[15] Brock, I don't know how, and I don't know when, but God will honor you for this."

God answers prayer.

Miracle Provision

God has continued to be true to his promise in Psalm 84:11, "The Lord will withhold no good thing from those who do what is right." In Brock's senior year, he earned multiple prestigious awards. We had been praying that somehow God might be mentioned at his public-school graduation, and it was accomplished through Brock's leadership bio.

Brock went on to attend a junior college that he selected because he believed God wanted him to play at a higher level, and junior college was a second run at that Division I goal. He also chose that college because the coach was a committed believer and mentored his players. Brock helped teach a Bible study for eighteen months while attending an apologetics course at Biola, and he fell in love with defending his faith.

Being a six-foot quarterback meant he needed a miracle to get a scholarship—one he really needed. Finally, the coach from Liberty University phoned his junior college coach to confirm Brock's talent and character. We had never seen our son as excited as when he signed that letter of intent.

God answers prayer!

A Godly Wife

A bigger smile and more excitement were just around the corner! Since before our son's birth, we had prayed for his future bride. When Brock had been at Liberty just a few days, I spoke in Phoenix and did a book

---

15. 1 Samuel 2:30, personalized.

signing for a Christian bookstore. While there, I struck up a conversation with the bookstore owner and his wife. Sheryl asked me, "Where did you say Brock got his scholarship?"

"He's the quarterback of Liberty University."

"My Hannah goes to Liberty!"

We gave the kids each other's phone numbers, and our two strong-willed, first-born kids decided to go on a date! After eighteen months of dating, and after they spent a week in fasting and prayer, Brock took Hannah on a tour of their relationship. At the place they first met, he gave her nails. At the place they first talked seriously, he gave her a hammer. At the place they first prayed together, he gave her a piece of wood. And at the home where she was living with her friends, he gave her a second piece of wood, which they hammered together to form a cross.

He knelt on one knee next to the cross and said, "Hannah, I love you. I want our relationship to start at the foot of the cross. Hannah, will you marry me? Hannah, can I kiss you?"

Hannah replied, "YES!"

Soon Brock and Hannah tied the knot.

God answers prayer.

One of our biggest prayers for our family is that we'd leave a legacy of love.

Everyday Leader

One of our biggest prayers for our family is that we'd leave a legacy of love. As newlyweds, we prayed that God would break the chains of chaos and dysfunction in our family tree. Brock has been a football coach and educator for nearly two decades. At the writing of this book, he is a teacher and head football coach at a large public school. He was honored as his state's high school football coach of the year, an award given, in part, for his unique character-building way of coaching.

He and his bride faithfully serve their local church, and all three of their children (our grandkids) love Jesus with their whole hearts. Because they also grasp the bigger picture of why and how God brought them together, they graciously allow us to tell their love story and the myriad of answered prayers that declare: "God honors those who honor him."

PAM FARREL is the mom of three sons (so her van usually smelled like a locker room). She is the author of sixty books (that helped pay for all those groceries that her athlete sons and their friends consumed steadily) and Nana to seven grandchildren (who love visiting her and Papa on the live-aboard boat they now call home). **Love-Wise.com**

From Nest to Next

Michelle Rayburn

WHAT IF ADULT CHILDREN ASKED their moms to write personal ads for them? Perhaps, one might read something a little like this:

> Single adult college student seeks first girlfriend to get his mother off his back. I have my own car, but it broke down, and my brother hasn't had a chance to take a look at it. I hope you don't mind taking the city bus on our dates. Or maybe you could drive. I'm almost finished with my college degree, and I'll be moving into my parents' basement soon. I work a campus job right now. I have a bushy beard. Deal with it. When I am home on spring break, I help my mom by cleaning the bathroom and emptying the dishwasher if she asks me enough times. I call myself laid back; she calls me lazy. I would rather read a book than worry about dishes. I like to wear plaid shorts with a flannel shirt. So? I'm looking for a girl who isn't bossy and won't tell me how to dress or where to spend my money. If you can be all of those things and deal with my mother, who wrote this ad for me, give me a call.

Full disclosure here: I really did write a similar ad when my son was in college, but it was part of a humorous Mother's Day feature published in a magazine under a pseudonym—for obvious reasons. So, before you think I deserve the horrible mother of the year award, let me clarify. My son was and is a wonderful guy. He is frugal to the core and made it through college debt-free by doing things like taking city busses and living at home for his student teaching semester (both of our boys did that). He's always been sort of the lumberjack professor type, which is part of his charm. And he found himself a wonderful wife a few years later without any intervention from me, thank goodness!

I wrote it with complete humor in my heart and with no malice. But if you're a mother of an adult son, you know there's also a dash of truth hidden in the flavors. It's like a marinara sauce that has a spice you can't place. What is that mingling with the basil and garlic and oregano? Is that a hint of fennel?

There is a weird transition time that comes when our boys are in college and on their own but sort of not on their own at the same time.

There is a weird transition time that comes when our boys are in college and on their own but sort of not on their own at the same time. And mingled with our parental support for their independence, ambition, and dreams, an outsider might perceive a hint of tension. It's the spicy result of trying to redefine boundaries and reestablish a new dynamic.

Acknowledge the Tension

During the time when our sons had one foot in and the other out of the nest, I asked myself often, "What's my role?" If we ask a twenty-something-year-old son to help with a task around the house and he doesn't do it, we can't exactly ground him or take away his PlayStation. I can't take the keys for the car he has paid for and fills with unleaded every week. Let's say he handles his own daily living activities for most of the year. When he's home on summer break, then what? Should he have chores? What are the consequences for not doing said chores?

I can't take the keys for the car he has paid for and fills with unleaded every week.

Although I wanted to take a hard-nosed, my-house-my-rules approach, that wasn't really fitting for our situation either. Most of the time, both of our boys were helpful and considerate during any stretches when they lived at home after high school. I also tried to put myself in their shoes because I once *was* in their shoes. I had struggled when I came home on college breaks to go back to curfews, house rules, chores, and family meals.

There have been times when one of our sons has invited our input on a big life decision as well as other times when I've nosed in and offered unsolicited advice that I should have kept to myself. Parenting a young adult son is a tense time of watching him become a man who is preparing to have his own home while he sometimes makes rookie mistakes or regresses back to resembling his junior high self.

He can write an impressive research paper and play a round of Nerf tag with his friends all in the same week—or same day. He can get a promotion at his part-time job for outstanding organization skills while living in a dorm room that brings him within one degree of separation from an episode of *Hoarders* where someone finds a cat carcass under pile of laundry and pizza boxes. Hyperbole? Boy moms, you know I'm not kidding here.

Decommission the Helicopter

From the time they were small, I reminded myself that my job was to raise and release. I knew that when boys marry, they regularly spend holidays with their wife's parents. Their traditions often center around her traditions. Not always. But often. And I knew that it's messy for a wife when a boy mom can't let go. I didn't want to be *that* mother-in-law. So, I prepared my heart for letting go. Any helicopter parenting habits had to be decommissioned before they graduated from high school.

In an ideal world, they would have never got off the ground and had flight. But I live in a real world, and I'm as good a parental helicopter pilot as any.

As comforting as it might have been to receive daily texts from my boys while they were away for college, I knew I didn't need to be involved in every decision or know about everything they did each day. Communication frequency was best left on their terms. They needed to learn how to problem-solve their own challenges and learn when to ask for help rather than relying on me to handle it all for them.

They needed to learn how to problem-solve their own challenges and learn when to ask for help rather than relying on me to handle it all for them.

The decommissioning began in junior high with forgotten assignments. Both of my boys had a habit of forgetting to return important homework to school after it was finished. I'd get phone calls asking if I could run a math worksheet or a forgotten science project to school. At first, I charged by the mile if I had to run to school to drop something off.

But then the financial impact didn't have much effect on the frequency of requests. (Gas prices were much lower then.) So, I said I would no longer cover for them. They would have to bring their work to school or take a failing grade. I *did* have grace a few times. Or was it mercy? Anyway, they learned to find methods of making sure it got in a backpack or by the door for the next morning.

In high school, the challenge for one son was getting out of bed to his own alarm. In his senior year, I began imagining future professors and bosses dealing with tardiness or absences when I would no longer be there to do wakeup duty. It was time to change the pattern. We had an exchange student living with us at the time who depended on the ride to school with host-bro. So, we set clear expectations. I would drive our exchange student to school if our son overslept, but I would not do any more wakeup calls. I would also not write fake excuses for tardiness. The consequences would be on him.

You know how this went, don't you?

Yep.

On morning of the first incident in Project Wake-Yourself, I drove our exchange student to school and was on my way back when I met my son in his car, heading toward school. We did not exchange pleasant waves on the road. Instead, he tried to sear a hole through my windshield with a glare.

Nurture Problem-Solving Skills

Once. My son was late for school only once after I refused to wake him anymore. He set up a genius system on his own where he had two alarm clocks. One was up on his bunkbed, and he set it to allow leeway to hit snooze a few times. He liked to give his brain a slower wake-up rather than an abrupt jarring. I get it. Me too!

He set up a second alarm clock on a dresser across the room that would require his getting down from the bunk to turn it off. This eliminated the possibility of accidentally turning off the alarm instead of hitting snooze. It's amazing what kids can come up with when given a challenge!

My default in this type of situation is often, "Here's what you need to do." But when left to their own problem-solving, it's surprising what my sons have come up with. It not only nurtures problem-solving but responsibility as well. If they come up with the plan, it isn't my fault if it doesn't work. Self-accountability is a beautiful thing.

Celebrate Both Progress and the Future

When I glance back at the years between our nest and their next, it's hard not to see some regrets in the memories. Nothing about parenting is perfect. It's a big experiment that mixes diverse personalities into one big unit. Conflict is part of growing.

Now that they are parents themselves, I have so much respect for my sons as fathers. I love watching their unique parenting styles emerge and hearing their little ones say, "Da-da!" Rather than looking at my own regret, I look forward with respect. Successes are not about what I did right but about how we're all right over time.

There is still a lot of communication between Dad and the boys about things they would never discuss with me. I'm ok with that secret code between men. Dad gets the calls about cracked sewer pipes, malfunctioning lawnmowers, and broken-down cars.

You know what never changes? I'm still the one they call in the what-should-I-do moments. I've heard the quiver in a son's voice when his child is miserable, and he doesn't know what to do. When a little one has a fever that won't break, or they need someone to run for more cough syrup and electrolytes. When they have questions about types of home loans and property tax.

We've all grown. But we won't outgrow needing each other. Someday, those problem-solving skills will come full circle, and they'll make care decisions for me. I'm confident they'll do just fine. They learned from a pro.

MICHELLE RAYBURN is an author and podcast host who helps others find hope in the trashy stuff of life. She has an MA in ministry leadership and writes Christian living books, humor, and Bible studies. Together with her husband, they've raised two sons and gained two daughters-in-law—plus three granddaughters (go estrogen team!) and a grandson. Dark chocolate, an iced coffee, and a good book in the hammock top Michelle's favorites list. **michellerayburn.com**

Final Thoughts

DEAR MOMS OF BOYS, I hope these stories serve as a gentle reminder that amid the chaos and noise, you are not alone. We've laughed, cried, and navigated the uncharted territories of raising these wild-hearted creatures together—some wilder than others. Embrace the mess, cherish the adventures, and revel in the extraordinary privilege of being a mom to your incredible sons. Let's applaud the beautiful chaos and the endless love that defines our journey as mothers of boys.

As we close, I'd love to offer a prayer over you:

> Heavenly Father,
>
> We have hearts full of gratitude to you, brimming with love for our precious boys. I humbly ask you to shower your divine blessings on the boy mom holding this book. In her role as a nurturer, guide, and source of unwavering love, I ask that you give her strength and wisdom to navigate the joys and challenges that accompany raising her sons.
>
> Bless her with patience, Lord, for there will be moments that test her resolve. Give her the ability to see beyond the mess and chaos and instead see the beauty in the unique young men entrusted to her care.
>
> Bless her compassionate heart, enabling her to instill kindness, empathy, and integrity in the hearts of her sons. May she be a beacon of love and acceptance, teaching them the value of treating others with dignity and respect.

Equip her with discernment as she guides her boys along their individual paths. Help her to recognize their strengths, encourage their passions, and nurture their dreams, so they may grow into the men you have destined them to be.

Wrap this devoted boy mom in your grace, Lord, shielding her from doubt, worry, and fatigue. Surround her with a supportive community that uplifts her spirit, provides comfort in times of need, and celebrates the triumphs and joys of motherhood. Surround her sons with your courage and shield them from harm, preparing them to face any adversity that comes their way. Maybe they walk confidently in the path you have laid before them.

Above all, Father, I ask for your abounding love and protection over this remarkable boy mom. Help her find solace in knowing that you walk alongside her every step of the way, offering strength when she is weak, wisdom when she is uncertain, and a boundless wellspring of love that knows no end. In your holy name, I pray. Amen.

THANK YOU TO EACH MOM who contributed a story to this book. You opened the door to your lives for us. Thank you for your vulnerability and humor. I'm honored to share the pages with you.

READER, DO YOU NEED MORE encouragement and inspiration? You'll notice that almost every writer has shared a book, website, podcast, or social media connection in her bio. If you find them online and subscribe to their email lists, read articles and books, and listen to podcast episodes, you'll discover even more support for the boy-mom life. We're here for you.

Michelle Rayburn

We would appreciate your review of *Life in the Estrogen-Free Zone* on your favorite book retailer's website!

If you enjoyed this book, you might also like the following collection of 34 stories from FCL Books, compiled and edited by Michelle Rayburn.

Life Repurposed: Stories of Grace, Hope, and Restored Faith

Print, E-book, Audiobook

Made in the USA
Monee, IL
18 July 2023